Ships of the Panama Canal

Ships of the Panama Canal

By James L. Shaw

Naval Institute Press   Annapolis, Maryland

Library of Congress Cataloging-in-Publication Data
Shaw, James L., 1943–
   Ships of the Panama Canal.
   Contains photographs taken by Ernest Hallen from
1907 to 1939, with text by James L. Shaw.
   Bibliography: p.
   Includes index.
   1. Warships—Panama—Panama Canal. 2. Warships—
Panama—Panama Canal—Pictorial works. 3. Ships—
Panama—Panama Canal. 4. Ships—Panama—Panama Canal—
Pictorial works. 5. Panama Canal (Panama)—Description.
6. Panama Canal (Panama)—Description—Views. I. Hallen,
Ernest. II. Title.
V767.S47   1985   387.2′097287′5   85-21611
ISBN 0-87021-629-5

Printed in the United States of America

For
Blanche Itasca Whallon

Contents

Acknowledgments

While this book is basically a collection of historical photographs, a good deal of research was required to provide pertinent background material for the many vessels involved. The scope of subject matter, ranging from well-known battleships and passenger liners to everyday cargo vessels and work craft, required a large network of correspondents. Of these, I must single out Mrs. Nan S. Chong of the Panama Canal Commission Library at Balboa, Panama, as a major contributor to this work. Mrs. Chong's extensive research into Panama Canal and Panama Railroad reports was instrumental in turning up facts not presented before in other publications. Likewise, I must thank Willie K. Friar, Pandora G. Aleman, Carolyn H. Twohy, Barbara A. Fuller, and Cleveland C. Soper III of the Panama Canal Commission for their very valuable assistance.

At the National Archives in Washington, D.C., where much of the historical material on the Panama Canal is found, I was given guidance by Jim Tremble and Barbara Burger. Mary Alice Kline of the United States Office of Personnel Management provided gov-

ernment records concerning Ernest Hallen's employment as official photographer of the Panama Canal. In tracing the history of the ships that crossed Panama well over four decades ago, I am indebted to Laura F. Brown and Ann House of the University of Baltimore's library housing the Steamship Historical Society of America Collection, Baltimore, Maryland; Charlotte Valentine of The Mariners' Museum, Newport News, Virginia, and Irene A. Stachura of the San Francisco Maritime Museum in California.

In the United Kingdom, H. S. Appleyard, K. O'Donoghue, J. J. Colledge, and D. J. Lees of the World Ship Society's Central Record provided invaluable research on vessel ownership transfers and movements. Historical information on ships of the United States Army and Navy was furnished by P. H. Silverstone, Christopher C. Wright, and Howard W. Serig, Jr. In the realm of sailing ships I was ably assisted by Capt. H. D. Huycke, Jr., Charles S. Morgan, Andrew Nesdall, and Rick Hogben. John E. Lingwood provided specific information on ships of the Pacific Steam Navigation Company, while

Fred Stindt helped cover the Matson Navigation Co., and Prof. John H. Kemble assisted with the Pacific Mail Steamship company.

Details concerning ships of the Union Steam Ship Company of New Zealand were supplied by J. A. Henry, while June Foster helped with Clan Line, and Dave Jones brought up several details concerning vessels of the Canadian Pacific. I must thank Karen Cooper for her assistance in assembling reference sources. Lloyd Stadum of Seattle, Washington, graciously reviewed material collected on the "535"- and "502"-class ships, while E. S. Blutecher, Dr. G. Spazzapan, Frank A. Clapp, and J. G. van Delden provided information on Norwegian, Italian, Canadian, and Dutch flag vessels.

The many people at the Naval Institute Press, Annapolis, especially Carol Swartz and Dick Hobbs, deserve special thanks for the attention and care given to this work. A. D. Baker III was overall reviewer of the manuscript, and his extraordinary knowledge of maritime history was essential in weeding out errors and tying up loose ends. Adrien M. Bouche, Jr., who rescued the Panama Canal glass plate collection twenty years ago, played an important part in identifying a number of "mystery" negatives. Mr. Bouche is now actively engaged in setting up a museum in the United States that will offer exhibits covering both the construction and operation of the Panama Canal. Last, but not least, I must thank my wife, Sheilagene, for her many hours of proofreading, indexing, and overall support.

1

Introduction

The photographs presented in this book were taken at the Panama Canal between the years 1907 and 1939. They are the product of a request made in 1906 by Panama Canal Engineer F. A. Maltby that photographs be taken of the construction work at Panama as it was accomplished. Mr. Maltby felt such illustration would be beneficial in formalizing progress reports and engineering plans. The man hired to photograph the canal was Ernest "Red" Hallen, a 32-year-old professional photographer who had arrived on the isthmus in January of 1906.

The new photographer was taken on to make purely technical prints; human interest was the last consideration. For the next eight years, Red Hallen climbed over, under, and around construction work at Panama to record with his camera every phase and detail of progress on the new waterway. Considering the bulky equipment he had to work with and the tropical rains and high humidity surrounding his subject, the results were exceptional. Today the Panama Canal Commission and the National Archives of the United States have a complete collection of photographs and negatives on file

illustrating almost every facet of canal construction. When the canal was finally opened for business in August of 1914, Red Hallen was again on hand to record the first ships to transit. Thereafter, ship photography became a very insignificant part of Hallen's daily work load. The visit of a newsworthy liner or an important warship might send him down to the locks on specific assignment, but usually, vessels were only photographed by chance, typically when he was at the canal on another project.

It was at these times, while he was waiting for some engineering work to be accomplished or dredging equipment to come into view, that Hallen would turn his camera on the passing commercial traffic of the day. In this manner, many common cargo carriers of the period, which would otherwise have gone unphotographed, were captured on glass plate. The irregularity of Hallen's ship photography is shown by the fact that on a single day, 15 September 1921, six photographs of transiting commercial ships were taken at Pedro Miguel Locks within minutes of each other; on the other hand, only four Hallen ship photographs have been found for

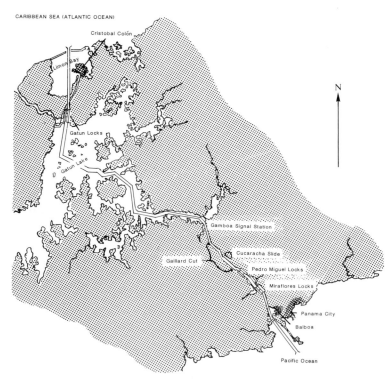

CARIBBEAN SEA (ATLANTIC OCEAN)

Cristobal Colón

Limon Bay

Gatun Locks

Gatun Lake

N

Gamboa Signal Station

Cucaracha Slide

Gaillard Cut

Pedro Miguel Locks

Miraflores Locks

Panama City

Balboa

Pacific Ocean

The Panama Canal

the year 1929, one for the year 1916, and none at all for the years 1936 and 1937.

Because of their importance and news appeal, early transits of U.S. Navy ships were frequently recorded. In 1919, while Red Hallen was on holiday in New York, it was announced that a major portion of the U.S. fleet was to move through Panama from the Atlantic to the Pacific. Realizing the significance of this first great naval transit of the canal, Red volunteered to return there on his own time to photograph the event. When he could not find a commercial sailing available, the navy pro-

vided him a berth on the destroyer *Ward*. Hallen arrived on the isthmus with the fleet and immediately set out with his equipment for the best vantage points, capturing most of the ships on film as they passed through. When the navy stationed its own photographer on the isthmus, Red's photography of naval ships became much less frequent.

Running on a northwest-southeast axis through jungle-clad mountains and across two lakes, the Panama Canal offered an intriguing backdrop for cameramen of the day. Ernest Hallen was quick to identify and establish the most promising places for ship photography. The locks were natural locations, providing close-up views of ships as they were held almost motionless while being raised or lowered from sea to sea. In his ship photography, Hallen seems to have held a preference for Pedro Miguel Locks. This may have been because of the site's proximity to Gaillard Cut. With a car at his disposal, Hallen could easily photograph a vessel from several points in the cut, then drive down to the ferry crossing at Pedro Miguel for a close-up as the ship locked through.

Gaillard Cut, where the canal had been excavated through Panama's continental divide, was the premier spot for views showing ships steaming across the isthmus. Unless dredges were at work, the cut was devoid of human activity, and transiting vessels were alone with the elements. From the heights afforded by the cut, and in particular Contractor's Hill, panoramas akin to aerial photography could be accomplished with the ships transiting majestically below. This was where Red Hallen chose to record some of the first commercial transits of the waterway, with dredges in the background fighting to keep back the ever-encroaching

Construction of locks at Pedro Miguel on the Pacific side during 1912.

3

slides. Many of Hallen's prints contain views of Cucaracha Slide, one of the canal's most notorious walls of moving earth. Even during the French period, this mound of rubble caused problems, and it continued to plague the canal well after construction was finished.

Other locations along the water passage offered different perspectives of shipping, and Hallen managed to make use of almost all of them. At Cristóbal, on the Atlantic side of the isthmus, he would photograph ships unloading and loading at the port's long finger piers, taking on fuel at the coaling wharf, or undergoing repairs in the small dry dock. A few miles away, at Gatun Locks, a tall lighthouse provided the perfect platform for elevated views of lock operation, something that was unavailable at the Pacific locks of Pedro Miguel and Miraflores. At the settlement of Paraiso, a short distance from Pedro Miguel, Hallen would climb up the booms of giant floating cranes to capture passing ships, the resulting view looking similar to what might be expected from a low-flying aircraft.

Outside of its humid weather during the rainy season, the Panama Canal offered the perfect environment for ship photography—the supply of shipping was endless, from an average of 3 ships a day in 1915, to over 14 a day in 1937, the last year Hallen was the canal's official photographer.

After Red Hallen retired and left the isthmus in 1937, his camera was handed over to his assistant, Manuel Smith, who continued to use glass-plate photography until late 1939. By the time plastic film came into official use at the canal during World War II, over 16,000 glass-plate negatives had been exposed, several hundred dating all the way back to a small collection left by the French construction project at Panama. Once the required photographs were printed, most of these plates were stacked away and forgotten.

In 1964, 17 years after Hallen's death, another canal employee, Adrien Bouché, Jr., remembered the plates and made it his task to go through them one by one, sorting, cleaning, indexing, and repairing as he went. The task took four years of part-time effort. In this quest, approximately 600 of the plates were discovered to contain views of shipping, either in the background or as the featured subject. Some dated back to views of Cristóbal and Balboa before the canal was completed; others were taken just a few months before the outbreak of World War II. While most plates were identified by date and description, a good portion were not. In the case of several plates involving transiting ships, the date given was found to be incorrect when cross-referenced against published Panama Canal transit records. In at least one case a ship itself was improperly identified. Considering the lengthy process of plate exposure and development, it is probable that dates were written on the negatives several days or perhaps even weeks after the actual event was photographed. For reasons known only to the photographer, a number of plates were never dated. It has been possible however, to establish a probable time period for many of these views by comparing background scenery in similar dated pictures and going back to the canal transit records for verification.

When Adrien Bouché, Jr., completed his indexing project, the majority of the glass plates were shipped off to the National Archives in Washington, D.C., where they remain on file today. A smaller collection of 2,230 plates was retained by the Panama Canal's Graphic Branch at Balboa. In addition, a chronological index was compiled of the Graphic Branch collection, giving a short description of each plate and its original identification number. The author made several trips to Washington and Balboa, Panama, to examine microfilm copies and bound volumes of both collections. This book is a compilation of the best of the surviving plates, chosen on the basis of print quality and historical interest.

A Note on Tonnages

Tonnage figures for commercial vessels in this book have been given in gross registered tons unless otherwise stated. A registered ton is a volume measurement of 100 cubic feet. The gross registered tonnage of a vessel is a measure of all permanently enclosed space available above and below decks for cargo, stores, and accommodation, with certain exceptions such as wheelhouse, chart room, radio room, etc. A net registered ton, on which Panama Canal transit tolls are charged, is the earning space of a ship, i.e., the gross tonnage less the crew's accommodation, ballast tanks, engine room, workshops, steering gear, anchor working space, and so forth. This definition of gross and net tonnage differs slightly among the world's major canals, the end result being that Panama tolls are higher than the others.

Tonnage figures for military vessels have been given in displacement tons unless otherwise stated. The displacement tonnage of a vessel is equivalent to the weight of water displaced by the ship and is thus the actual weight of the ship. A load displacement ton, on which Panama Canal transit tolls for warships are charged, is the ship's weight when fully loaded, i.e., with all crew, effects, stores, and fuel on board. During the time period covered, merchant vessels carrying passengers or cargo (to include army and navy transports, colliers, hospital ships, and supply ships) through the Panama Canal were charged a transit toll of $1.20 for each net vessel ton of 100 cubic feet of actual earning capacity based on Panama Canal measurement. Vessels in ballast, without passengers or cargo, were charged $0.72 for each net vessel ton. Warships were charged $0.50 per load displacement ton. However, tolls could not exceed the equivalent of $1.25 per net registered ton as determined by United States rules of measurement, nor be less than the equivalent of $0.75 per net U.S. registered ton. To give some idea of how the various "tons" came into play at the canal, several vessel transits can be examined in detail.

In April 1920 the cargo vessel *Cajacet* arrived at Balboa with 9,730 long tons (or 21,795,200 pounds) of nitrate on board. The ship itself measured 3,567 net tons under United States registration measurement (it had 356,700 cubic feet of revenue-earning storage space available). Going under the regulations then in force, the *Cajacet* was assessed a transit toll of $4,458.75 (its U.S. net tonnage of 3,567 times the maximum transit charge per net ton of $1.25). This worked out to a fee of 46.85 cents per ton of cargo, one of the lowest recorded up to that time. In 1927 the French tug *Nembrou*, sailing from Dunkirk to New Caledonia in ballast, transited the canal free of charge owing to the proviso that, while a vessel in ballast should be charged 72 cents per net ton under Panama Canal measurement, the sum total could not exceed $1.25 per net ton under the rules of measurement for registry in the United States. In admeasuring the *Nembrou*, it was found that the propelling power space, increased by 75 percent of itself, together with all other legitimate deductions for crew, navigation spaces, etc., comprised a sum of deductions greater than the

Steam shovels and dirt trains at the bottom of Gaillard Cut on 28 December 1912.

gross tonnage which, from a mathematical standpoint, occasioned a negative tonnage. In consequence of this condition, the Panama Canal net tonnage times 72 cents was greater than the maximum allowed (zero × $1.25), and hence no tolls were collectible.

While a merchant vessel would usually retain its net registered ton measurement (unless structurally altered), and thus face the same Panama Canal toll on successive transits regardless of the amount of cargo carried (unless in ballast), a warship was assessed tolls on total ship weight, a figure that would almost always be different on each visit. In February of 1931 the British battleship *Nelson* transited the canal from the Atlantic to visit the U.S. Pacific Fleet then anchored off Balboa. The *Nelson* had been built to a "standard" displacement of 33,313 tons as defined by the Washington Treaty of 1922. However, when it arrived at Panama with crew, equipment, and provisions on board, it had a load displacement of 36,640 tons. At $0.50 per load displacement ton, the British warship was assessed a transit toll of $18,320. Yet on its return to the Atlantic, after a small amount of fuel and provisions had been consumed at Balboa, the ship displaced 36,494 tons, thus it paid a slightly lower toll of $18,247.

A Brief History of the Panama Canal

Though the dream of an interocean waterway through the Central American isthmus has been traced back as far as the early Spanish explorations of the sixteenth century, it was not until the middle of the nineteenth century that the technological means to build such a canal, along with sufficient capital for its construction, were available. Two events then turned the eyes of the world to the narrow isthmus—the California Gold Rush of 1849, which funneled thousands of prospectors across Panama and Nicaragua to the Pacific, and the digging of the Suez Canal, which, when completed, exhibited to the world the potential of connecting oceans by a man-made waterway. The time was right to begin turning the dream of an interocean passage through the Americas into reality.

Also during this period, ship design—and shipbuilding technology—had reached very significant stages in their evolution. In 1843 the first of the big screw-propelled steamships built of iron, the 3,270-ton *Great Britain*, was launched in England. From here on out ships were to increase in size—first slowly, and then so rapidly that canal designers would be hard put to keep pace. In 1858, one year before Ferdinand de Lesseps and his engineers started work on the Suez Canal in Egypt, Isambard Kingdom Brunel launched his enormous

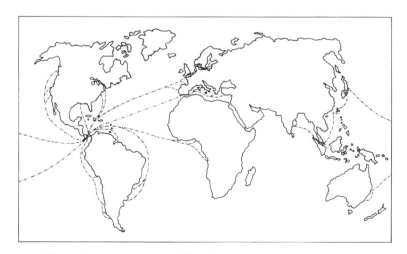

World trade routes served by the Panama Canal.

18,915-ton steamship *Great Eastern*. Though an oddity of her times, and not to be surpassed in size until the turn of the century, the 691-foot by 83-foot *Great Eastern* gave proof that the construction and operation of very large vessels was possible. This was a fact that future canal planners would have to take into consideration.

The first man to draw up a legitimate plan for an interocean canal across Central America was Orville Childs, an American engineer employed by Cornelius Vanderbilt. During the California Gold Rush, Vanderbilt operated one of several steamship companies funneling prospectors to the Pacific by way of the Central American isthmus. His ships traveled between the United States and Greytown, Nicaragua, where they unloaded their passengers at the mouth of the San Juan del Norte river. At Greytown, Vanderbilt's gold seekers took boats up the river to Lake Nicaragua, crossed the lake by steamer, then continued on to the Pacific by stagecoach and muleback.

Under Vanderbilt's direction, Childs drew up designs for a lock-type canal, which would have made use of Nicaragua's centrally located lake and the relatively straight course of the San Juan del Norte River. His plan called for the construction of a canal using 28 lock chambers, 14 on the Atlantic coast and 14 on the Pacific coast, each lock stepping a ship up or down a maximum of eight feet. The locks would measure 250 feet in length and 60 feet in width, with a depth of 17 feet. The canal's channel width would be 50 feet, extended to 90 feet at turns, and its total length would be 194.4 miles. Excavation would proceed through a mountain pass measuring only 153 feet above sea level that Childs had discovered on the Pacific coast.

The measurements of Child's canal were thought

Ernest "Red" Hallen (1875–1947), official photographer at the Panama Canal from 1907 to 1937.

adequate for the day, even though the *Great Britain*, which had already been launched in England, measured over 300 feet in length. Vanderbilt's ships would certainly fit through, as would all vessels then trading to the isthmus. The tapering off of the Gold Rush, however, and the completion of the Panama Railroad in 1855, sounded the death knell for Vanderbilt's Nicaraguan canal. Few saw any future need for such a complicated and costly structure.

The Panama Railroad was to play an extremely important part in the eventual completion of an interocean canal through the Americas. It had been launched during the whirlwind of the California Gold Rush. William Henry Aspinwall, an influential backer of the railroad, was also a shipping man. He had created the Pacific Mail Steamship Company in 1848. In 1855 the

Panama Railroad linked the port of Aspinwall on the Caribbean with Panama City on the Pacific. With the provision of adequate steamship service to both ports by vessels of the Pacific Mail Steamship Company, Pacific Steam Navigation Company, and the Royal Mail Steam Packet Company, pressure to build an interocean canal was dissipated.

It was not until the 1870s, shortly after the Suez Canal had been successfully completed, that a second plan to cross Central America by canal was formulated. U.S. Navy Commander Edward P. Lull, who had surveyed both Panama and Nicaragua on U.S. government-sponsored expeditions, submitted the design. Lull's project, drawn up in 1873, again called for a lock canal across Nicaragua, eleven locks up and ten locks down, with Lake Nicaragua to be used as a natural "water bridge" across the continent. Lull's lock chambers measured 400 feet by 70 feet and were 26 feet deep. These dimensions reflected the advances that had been made in shipbuilding during the intervening two decades. A British warship, the *Northumberland*, had been launched in 1868 with a length of slightly over 400 feet and a draft of 27 feet. But again, Lull's canal was not to be built for the biggest or potentially biggest ships. It was designed simply to serve the vessels then engaged or expected to be engaged in the trans-isthmus trade.

When an international congress was convened in Paris six years later to study the possible construction of an interocean waterway in Central America, the American position was presented by Aniceto García Menocal, who had assisted Edward Lull in formalizing the Nicaraguan plan. Menocal was convinced that a lock canal, as outlined by Lull, could be built across Nicaragua from the Caribbean to the Pacific for a cost of

$65,600,000. On the other hand, Menocal's minimum estimate for a lock canal across Panama, where high mountains and swollen rivers acted as barriers, was $94,000,000. A canal could also be built across the Tehauntepec Isthmus of Mexico, it was stated, but such a project would require a prohibitive 140 locks to lift ships over the 812-foot summit of the Tehauntepec mountains.

The French, now backed by a very interested and involved Ferdinand de Lesseps, proposed that a sea-level canal, incorporating a nine-mile-long tunnel through the mountains, could be built at Panama for approximately the same price as the American lock project. Disregarding the difficulties of Panama—the disease, the mountains, and the rivers—de Lesseps was sure that a second Suez could be constructed from the Atlantic to the Pacific in twelve years. The waterway's bottom width would be 79 feet with a depth of 29 feet, figures almost identical to those of Suez. Only in length and price were the two canals to differ. Panama would be shorter by 60 miles and was projected to cost almost three times as much.

Ironically, a third plan was presented at the congress, which was to haunt the ultimate French failure at Panama and, at the same time, point in the direction of the future American triumph. This was a proposal presented by a French government engineer, Baron Godin de Lepinay, for a canal in Panama. It was similar to the American plan for Nicaragua in which Lake Nicaragua was to be connected to both oceans by a series of locks. The lake would provide both a portion of the canal channel and the water by which to operate the locks. To build such a canal at Panama, the French engineer proposed damming the notorious Chagres river and a

Gaillard Cut at deepest excavation of canal between Gold Hill and Contractor's Hill in June of 1913.

smaller Pacific stream, the Rio Grande, to form two artificial lakes. These would be joined by a channel cut through the continental divide. Ships would be routed around the dams by a series of locks. The idea made sense, but it was given little credit. The French, under de Lesseps, insisted on a sea-level canal. The Americans wanted a Nicaraguan canal. There could be no compromise.

One American engineer of the period was not even sure that a canal was the solution. James B. Eads, a well-known bridge builder, proposed that a gigantic railway with the capacity to haul ships of up to 8,000-tons in massive cradles could be built across the isthmus of southern Mexico for much less than any man-made ditch at either Panama or Nicaragua. This idea was not

1. Tehauntepec
2. Nicaragua
3. Chirique
4. Panama
5. San Blas
6. Caledonia
7. Darien
8. Atrato

Main routes proposed for a canal across the Central American isthmus during surveys conducted between 1840–1900.

considered outrageous and, in fact, was given consideration again in a study of potential isthmian canal routes carried out as late as 1947.

The outcome of the Congress of 1879 was something of a foregone conclusion on the part of de Lesseps and his backers. They would proceed with the construction of a sea-level canal at Panama, a "second" Suez. The American engineers were left to roll up their plans for a lock canal across Nicaragua and return to New York. The French arrived at Panama the following year, 1880.

While de Lesseps and his engineers began work on the isthmus, the Americans revised their plans for a Nicaraguan canal, quite confident that the French effort would fail. In 1885 Menocal put forward an up-dated plan that featured four locks on the Pacific, each with a total lift of 33 feet, and three locks on the Atlantic, one providing as much as 53 feet of lift. The lock chambers were to measure 650 feet by 65 feet with a depth of 29 feet. The canal's total length would be 169.8 miles with a channel width of between 80 and 120 feet. At the time, this was felt to be quite sufficient to deal with expected shipping. Cunard's 8,127-ton liner *Umbria*, launched in 1884, measured 520 feet in length with a 57-foot beam and a draft of 25 feet. But she and others like her were not envisioned as clients of a Central American canal.

In the last few years of the de Lesseps project, when cost overruns threatened financial disaster, the French also embraced the idea of a lock canal as a means of cutting costs at Panama. French engineers drew up their own plans calling for a series of ten locks, five on the Pacific side and five on the Atlantic side. These would step ships up to a central lake 161 feet above sea level. The locks were to measure 590 feet by 59 feet with a depth of 29.5 feet, measurements deemed adequate for

11

most steamers of the day. The 10,499-ton Inman liners *City of New York* and *City of Paris* were being built by this time, each ship to measure 560 feet by 63 feet. In addition, a number of warships had already been put into service with beams exceeding 59 feet. But again, no reason could be seen for such giants to seek an isthmian passage. The canal was only to get the average commercial ship across the mountains, and no more.

As the French project at Panama dug itself deeper into debt, a company was formed in the United States to undertake what many Americans thought needed to be done in Central America. In 1889, the year that the French effort at Panama ground to a halt, the privately capitalized Maritime Canal Company was chartered to build a lock canal across Nicaragua. The plan to be used was a modified version of A. G. Menocal's 1885 design. Three locks with lifts of 31, 35, and 44 feet would be used on each side of the isthmus to step vessels up and down from a lake summit level of 110 feet. The lock chambers would measure 650 feet by 70 feet with a 28- to 30-foot depth. For those times a lock lift of 44 feet was without precedent, but it was felt that equipment to accomplish such a lift was now at hand.

Like the French before them, the Americans arrived on the isthmus in high hopes. Building were put up; storehouses, barracks, hospitals, shops, and offices were all constructed of wood, which was brought in from the United States. Five dredges and a number of tugs and barges were purchased from the defunct French company and towed north to the American site at Greytown. A railroad was built 11 miles inland to the location where the first two locks were to be constructed. Locomotives and flatcars were imported. The line of the canal would follow a nearly direct course from Greytown to just below the small settlement of San Carlos on the eastern shore of Lake Nicaragua. From there, ships would cross the lake, then be stepped down through locks to the Pacific. It was a grand scheme, but it failed even more miserably than the French project in Panama. By 1892 work had come to a complete halt. Money had run out, and only 727,861 cubic yards of soil had been moved. The buildings, the equipment, and the plans were left to rot in the jungle. For the next three years the Isthmus of Central America lay quiet. The jungle began reclaiming its own. Two attempts to cross the mountains had failed, resulting in a sprawling heap of abandoned equipment, ruined men, and thousands of graves. However, neither France nor the United States was yet willing to give up the battle.

On October 20, 1894, the Compagnie Nouvelle du Canal de Panama was incorporated in Paris to continue chipping away at the Panamanian cordillera. It was literally a "holding" company, set up to hold on to the French concession at Panama by continuing some work on the project, however small. Only a few pieces of equipment brought in by the first French company were kept in use. The remainder was either stored or abandoned. The new company was to mark time until new plans and new capital for a second assault could be obtained.

The Americans were also re-thinking their Nicaraguan project. The Nicaragua Canal Board, a group of qualified engineers and surveyors, was sent down to look over the Maritime Canal Company holdings and gauge what would be necessary to begin a second attempt. The team found little of the forlorn project worth saving. Several structures still stood, and portions of the railway line remained in usable condition, but all

Unfinished Gatun Locks looking towards the Atlantic on 16 March 1913.

five dredges lay in the harbor abandoned, their machinery rusting. The tugs and barges were beyond repair as was most of the railway rolling stock. Only the larger buildings and the machine shop seemed functional.

Although the Maritime Canal Company was quite willing to dispose of its meager holdings, it could furnish no accurate drawings of the locks it had intended to construct. The Nicaragua Canal Board, therefore, had to make cost estimates for continuing the Nicaragua canal by comparing the costs of other recently completed works, including the new Sault Ste. Marie Lock and the St. Marys Falls Canal. It was proposed that the originally contemplated six locks requiring excessive lifts be replaced with eight locks in two sets of four. In each case the chamber nearest the sea would have a lift of 26 feet from the level of mean tide, and the remaining three would have lifts of 28 feet each. As America had now entered the battleship race, the board recommended that the proposed canal's lock width be enlarged to 80 feet. The USS *Iowa*, with a beam of 72 feet 3 inches, had already been launched, and bigger ships were expected to follow.

The French were also reappraising their projected canal at Panama. A Comité Technique had been formed in 1896 to determine the best possible plan for continuing the work. In 1898 it released its findings, which called for a number of major modifications. There were to be two artificial lakes created, one at an elevation of 61.5 feet above sea level, the other at 97.5 feet above sea level. The lakes would be reached from the Atlantic side by four locks in two sets of two. On the Pacific side, one pair of two-flight locks and two single locks would be needed. The canal was to have a bottom width of 98 feet and a depth of 29.5 feet. Lock dimensions were to be 738 feet by 82 feet with a depth of 32 feet. Cost was estimated at $101,850,000. Basically, it was the canal proposed by the Frenchman Godin de Lepinay almost two decades earlier.

Before the Comité Technique released its report, however, the Spanish-American war took place, and the well-publicized race of the battleship USS *Oregon* around the tip of South America had turned American public opinion towards the completion of a transisthmus canal. The American victory in the war with Spain ushered in a new era for the United States, one laced with global possessions and responsibilities. A U.S. canal across Central America, to provide easy and quick access to the Pacific for its navy and merchant fleet, was suddenly a clear necessity. Though American public and political consensus continued to back Nicaragua as the location for an interocean canal, one of that country's most visible shortcomings was its volcanoes, several of which were active. As if to underscore this problem, a long-dormant volcano on the Caribbean island of Martinique, Mount Pelée, erupted on 8 May 1902, killing nearly 30,000 people in the city of St. Pierre. Though Nicaragua's volcanoes were over 1,500 miles to the west of Martinique, the eruption of Mount Pelée and its resulting catastrophic destruction quickly focused attention on Nicaragua's brooding mountains.

The volcanoes of Nicaragua were a prominent issue when the U.S. Congress sat down in 1902 to make a final decision on the location of a U.S.-controlled interocean waterway. A majority of legislators still favored Nicaragua, but the final vote was to be swayed by several important factors, only one of which was volcanoes. In a dramatic speech on the Senate floor, Senator Mark Hanna of Ohio, one of the most powerful politi-

Discarded French dredge in canal channel between Pedro Miguel and Miraflores on 5 July 1913.

cal influences on United States affairs of his time, came out in favor of the Panama route. Basing his argument purely on technical grounds, Hanna expounded the Panama route as having a shorter distance, requiring less locks and less curves and, therefore, one that would require less maintenence. Also mentioned was the fact that Panama had two good harbors, an operating railroad, and many supportive facilities already put in place by the French—facilities they were now willing to sell at a low price. When the final ballot was taken, the Panama route won by eight votes. Over the next two years the United States purchased the bankrupt French project at Panama for $40,000,000 and signed an agreement with the newly independent Republic of Panama for the rights to build an interocean canal between the Atlantic and the Pacific. The canal was to parallel closely the route covered by the Panama railroad.

The U.S. project at Panama began in late 1904 under the direction of John F. Wallace. By carefully weighed estimates, the American canal was expected to cost $247,000,000 and be completed in twelve to thirteen years—figures similar to what the French had come up with a quarter century earlier. Like the original French plan, it was to be a sea-level canal, but the dimensions were to be increased to a channel width of 150 feet and a depth of 35 feet. The larger measurements were brought about by a new generation of ships then under construction, including five new 15,000-ton American battleships of the *Virginia* class, which were being built with a beam of 76 feet 2 inches and a mean draft of 26 feet 8 inches.

Although European interests had long favored a sea-level canal at Panama, there was a minority opposition in the United States to such a project, particularly among those who had first-hand experience with the terrain along the projected route. This opposition was strengthened in 1905 when John Stevens, a railway engineer, replaced John F. Wallace as director of construction on the waterway and saw for himself the difficulties of pursuing such a canal at Panama. Stevens doubted that a sea-level canal could be finished before 1924, but he was sure that a lock canal could be pushed through by 1914 at a cost considerably below that estimated for a sea-level course. Theodore Roosevelt, who had become the president of the United States in 1901 following the assassination of William McKinley, stood firmly behind the concept of a sea-level canal, but he also wanted a canal quickly; indeed, the rapid completion of an interocean waterway was one of his main aims. Once the difficulties of a sea-level canal were explained to him by Stevens, he was fully prepared to accept the lock concept, especially if it meant a speedy and successful project. The U.S. Senate was skeptical, but when the final vote was taken on 19 June 1906, the lock concept was adopted by a vote of 36 to 31.

Once the issue of design was settled, work began in earnest at Panama. The new American plan, again essentially the same as had been proposed in 1879 by French engineer Godin de Lepinay, called for the creation of artificial lakes in the middle of Panama by the damming of the Chagres and Rio Grande rivers. Locks would then be used to step ships up and down between the lakes and the sea. Major excavation would be limited to a deep cut through Panama's mountainous interior. The plan itself was simple, but its eventual completion would require the conquering of disease, the clearing of jungle, and the movement of over 232-million cubic yards of earth and rock—enough material,

16

it was pointed out, to "build a tower with the dimensions of a city block nineteen miles into the air."

The remains of the French project at Panama, including the Panama Railroad, were taken over by the Americans. Though most of the equipment had not operated for several years, much of it was found to be well preserved, allowing a good portion to be put into immediate use. Hospitals that the French had built were acquired and a specialist in tropical diseases, William C. Gorgas, placed in charge. His battle with the elusive mosquito was to be just as courageous and just as important to the final American success at Panama as the work of the engineers and builders who labored to complete the project. John Stevens was responsible for the tremendous job of organizing construction at Panama. A railroad man, he saw that everything would need to be put in place before excavation could commence. He capitalized on the use of the Panama Railroad as a means of transporting canal spoils away from the work site, something the French had largely overlooked.

On 9 November 1906, President Teddy Roosevelt sailed for Panama on his first and only visit to the isthmus. The battleship *Louisiana*, escorted by the cruisers *Tennessee* and *Washington*, arrived off Colón, formerly Aspinwall, on November 14th. The president's visit, though brief, served to focus attention on what needed to be done on the project and roused the fervor of the canal workers to complete the work. In 1907, with work progressing satisfactorily, John Stevens stepped down as construction supervisor and a new man was appointed, Colonel George W. Goethals. Goethals, an army engineer, put a firm hand on the canal-building venture. It was after this transition that several major changes were made in the basic plan of the waterway.

The size of ships was still increasing. The U.S. Navy was considering the construction of a class of battleships with a beam of 94 feet. The British, already in possession of the *Lusitania* and *Mauretania*—each measuring 790 feet by 88 feet—were projecting even larger ocean liners for the North Atlantic run, as were the Germans. Though the prospect of these ships ever using the Panama Canal was slim, the language authorizing construction of the American waterway specifically called for a canal "of sufficient capacity and depth as shall afford convenient passage for vessels of the largest tonnage and greatest draft now in use, and such as may be reasonably anticipated." To accommodate these large vessels—and those "reasonably anticipated"—it was decided to make the bottom width of the cut through the mountain chain 300 feet wide, or almost four times as wide as the original French plans had called for. The lock chambers were also to be increased in size, from a width of 95 feet to 100 feet. Length of the locks would be set at 1,000 feet, enough to easily accommodate the largest of ships and sufficient to transit two smaller vessels at one time. At the suggestion of the navy, the lock width was increased again, to 110 feet, just before construction began.

Not all were in agreement on the size of the Panama Canal locks. President Roosevelt had called for a lock width of 120 feet in his annual message sent to Congress on 3 December 1907. Several canal engineers thought 125 feet would not be too wide, considering the advances being made in ship construction. Others were not quite sure that such large measurements were called for. Colonel Goethals doubted that the navy would ever

Spanish laborers removing tracks from Gaillard Cut on 4 September 1913.

build vessels requiring a lock wider than 100 feet. Other concerned persons pointed out that larger locks would require more water to operate them, thus reducing the canal's overall ship-handling capacity. But most thought that the 1,000-foot-by-110-foot measurements were entirely adequate and that the proposed dimensions would easily fulfill the terms of the language authorizing the canal.

A large labor force was assembled at Panama, the major part coming from the nearby Caribbean islands. Most skilled personnel were recruited from the United States, but others came from Europe, North and South America, Asia, and Africa. Before the canal was completed, a total of ninety-seven countries would be represented on the isthmus, making the building of the canal a truly international endeavor. Supplies to construct the canal and support its work force were funneled in at a rapid rate. On 1 July 1907, the SS *Haakon VII* arrived at Colón from New Orleans with 1,190 barrels of mosquito oil on board. The schooner *Edward* arrived from Barranquilla, Colombia, that same afternoon with 513 tons of brick. On July 5th the *Mobila* brought in shovels, furniture, and boilers. Six days later the SS *Santona* sailed in from Gulfport, Mississippi, with 4,680 pieces of piling. The arriving ships soon overwhelmed the limited docking facilities at Colón, but the cargo was unloaded. On July 13th the tug *Powerful* arrived from Newport News with three steel barges. A week later the SS *Mara Kolb* brought in three boilers, a steam hammer, six hoisting engines, and over 2,000 tons of steel plate. Animal power, in the form of mules and horses, was still being used on the isthmus. For their benefit the SS *Ellis* arrived from New Orleans on August 8th with 70 tons of hay and 40 tons of oats. On August

19th the steel dipper dredge *Mindi* arrived from Baltimore in tow of the tug *Jack Twohy*. The SS *Westhampton* followed on the 28th with 600 tons of dynamite and 918 tons of steel rail.

In 1905, to ferry the large number of workers required for the construction of the canal, the Isthmian Canal Commission had purchased two passenger steamers, the *Havana* and *Mexico*, which it had renamed *Panama* and *Colón*. These vessels were to be operated by the Panama Railroad Steamship Line. Two large cargo vessels, the *Shawmut* and *Tremont*, were purchased in 1908 to carry cement cargoes from New York to the canal. These ships were renamed *Ancon* and *Cristobal* and, unknown at the time, were to become the first oceangoing ships to pass through the completed canal.

Once disease was conquered on the isthmus through the successful efforts of William Gorgas, construction efforts were intensified. Work was centered at Culebra, where a massive cut was made between the mountains. When it came to breaking through the continental divide, dynamite was the chief resource of the engineers. Over 60,000,000 pounds of the explosive would be used in the digging of the canal, and almost half the work force was to be involved in at least some phase of transporting or placing the dangerous commodity. To remove the resulting rock and earth, a collection of 95-ton Bucyrus steam shovels was assembled. At the height of digging, in 1909, sixty-eight of these machines removed over two million cubic yards of material in one month, ten times the volume achieved by the French at their best. In fact, such was the extent of the American effort that once all equipment was in operation, the equivalent of a Suez Canal was being excavated every

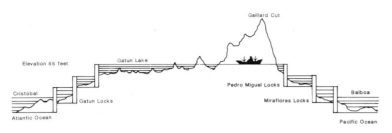

Panama Canal Profile

three years. To rid the construction site of spoils, approximately 160 dirt trains were operated in and out of the cut every day. Over 2,500,000 cubic feet of this material was used to build a breakwater on the Pacific side of the canal, but the largest proportion (23 million cubic yards) went into the construction of Gatun Dam, which would hold back the waterway's biggest artificial lake.

On 25 August 1909, the first concrete was poured at Gatun Locks. More than two million cubic yards of the material were used before the job was completed. Sand and gravel were obtained locally and brought to the construction site by barge and rail. On the Pacific side of the isthmus, at Miraflores and Pedro Miguel locks, huge cantilever cranes were used to lift buckets of mixed concrete over obstructions to the waiting timber forms. While concrete was poured, work was begun on the lock gates, the doors that would eventually open the Isthmus of Panama to the world's shipping. The lock gates were designed by Henry Goldmark. They were massive metal structures built in much the same manner as ships of the period, with steel plate riveted to a skeleton of steel girders. All the lock doors were 65-feet wide and 7 feet thick. They varied in height from 47 to 82 feet. The

tallest were positioned at the Pacific end of the Miraflores Locks where tidal variations were greatest (22 feet). Though weighing up to 745 tons, the gate leaves were built to virtually float in the water.

The entire lock system was to be operated by electricity. Indeed, it would be an "electric" canal. Electric motors produced by the General Electric Company would provide the power, while electric relays and switches exerted control. In all, over 1,500 electric motors operated the various mechanisms involved in the locks. Even the small locomotives that kept the ships in position while transiting the locks were electrically powered. This extensive use of the new "genie" of the twentieth century would not have been possible even a decade earlier. The locks at Pedro Miguel were finished in 1911, followed by Miraflores and Gatun locks in 1913. Excavation at Culebra had proceeded on schedule, and two steam shovels finally met head-to-head on 20 May 1913. The bottom of the canal at its highest point was 40 feet above sea level. On September 10th the last dirt train left the cut. The equipment that had dug its way across the continent was retired—much of it to be sent north to help in the construction of the Alaska Railroad—and miles of track that had supported the dirt trains was ripped up. On 10 October 1913, President Wilson pushed a button in the Executive Building in Washington, D.C., which was relayed to Panama by telegraph. The transmitted signal detonated dynamite in the Gamboa Dike, which held back the waters of Gatun Lake from Culebra Cut. In a few moments the isthmus was breeched by a new waterway, allowing dredges to take over the work of steam shovels.

Some 4,500,000 cubic yards of concrete had been poured to create the Panama Canal lock system, while over 200 million cubic yards of earth and rock had been excavated to create the channel. Dredges would now finish the work, including the removal of several large earth slides that had occurred during the digging operations. The Gatun lock system was tried for the first time on 26 September 1913 by the canal tug *Gatun*. The lock gates worked perfectly, and the small tug was able to complete its transit from sea level to the 85-foot elevation of Gatun Lake in less than two hours. On 24 October 1913, a convoy of workboats, barges, and dredges transited up through Miraflores and Pedro Miguel locks, becoming the first vessels to use the Pacific lock system. Without incident or celebration, an old crane boat left over from the French era, the *Alexandre La Valley*, which had come up through Gatun Locks to accomplish work in the main channel, passed down through the Pacific locks on 7 January 1914 and became the first vessel to transit the complete length of the waterway. Suddenly, the end of the great construction project was at hand.

In the United States, where construction of the canal had been followed by the public for almost a decade, plans had been made for a huge celebration to open the canal to world commerce. At least a hundred warships were to form a vast armada that would steam from Hampton Roads, Virginia, to San Francisco via the canal to demonstrate the waterway's strategic value. At San Francisco their arrival would signal the commencement of the Panama-Pacific International Exposition, a mammoth fair to be held to commemorate the canal's opening. Recommendations had even been made that the old battleship *Oregon*, which had first shown the need for an American interocean canal, lead the armada under the command of her retired captain. The sailing of the great armada was not to be, for in that same August, war broke out in Europe. It was not to be a powerful armada that would open the canal. Instead, the SS *Cristobal*, which had hauled much of the cement for the canal locks, became the first oceangoing vessel to transit the canal on 3 August 1914. On August 15th, the SS *Ancon* performed an official transit to open the canal, a journey accomplished in 9 hours and 40 minutes. The long-awaited opening, however, was almost forgotten in wake of the storm now breaking over civilization.

The American canal project at Panama, while successful, had been costly, even if completed in less time and under the budget first projected. No other effort, outside of war, had called for a higher expenditure of dollars and human lives. The final price, including the purchase of the French project and payments to Panama and Colombia, amounted to $352,000,000. If the money spent by the two French projects was added, the total cost of the Panama Canal was over $639 million. In human lives, American hospital records recorded 5,609 deaths due to accident and disease from 1904 to the canal's official opening. If lives lost during the French period were counted, however, the toll could be placed at well over 22,000.

A total volume of 232,440,945 cubic yards of excavation was accomplished at Panama by the Americans. The French before them had excavated 50,000,000 cubic meters, over half of which had been usefully incorporated into the American project. The final volume of dirt and rock removed from the canal's path was easily over four times the amount that de Lesseps had envisioned in his original plans for Panama. The labors at Suez paled in comparison with what had been accomplished at Panama, where a volume of dirt nearly equal to three Suez Canals had been removed. Yet, the Panama Canal was a product of its times. Technology and human resolve had arrived on the Central American isthmus in harmony and at the same time.

The world's shipbuilding industry was to take less than two decades to produce a vessel incapable of transiting the Panama Canal because of its size. On 29 October 1932, the 79,280-ton *Normandie* was launched at the French yard of Penhöet, St. Nazaire. The luxury liner measured 1,030 feet by 117.8 feet. Two years later the *Queen Mary*, measuring 1,019 feet by 118.1 feet, was launched by John Brown, Clydebank, in Great Britain.

In 1939, work was initiated on the "Third Locks Project" at Panama, which was to both increase the ability of the canal to transit larger ships and make it less vulnerable to air or naval attack. The chambers of the Third Locks were to be 1,200 feet long and 140 feet wide, with a navigable depth of 45 feet. An expenditure of $277,000,000 was authorized for construction. Of this, $75,000,000 was actually spent excavating the new locks at Miraflores and Gatun before the more pressing priorities of World War II halted the project in early 1942. The excavated channels for these locks, now flooded with water, remain in place today.

2

Naval Ships and Military Transports

When the French began work at Panama in 1880, the United States Navy was not the outstanding fighting force it is today. Even in the Western Hemisphere the navies of Argentina, Brazil, and Chile were regarded as superior. This situation changed in the mid-1880s when the U.S. Congress, reacting to the modernization of Latin American fleets, authorized construction of two new seagoing armored fighting ships, the *Texas* and *Maine*, which were to become America's first battleships. The keels for these two vessels were laid down in 1888 and 1889, the same years in which the first French canal project at Panama faltered. Both vessels were commissioned in 1895. While larger, faster, and more heavily armed than their Latin American contemporaries, the U.S. warships were still much smaller than the capital vessels of most European navies.

In 1890, the year in which Alfred Mahan's book *The Influence of Sea Power upon History* first appeared, a further three U.S. battleships, the *Indiana, Massachusetts,* and *Oregon* were authorized. The *Oregon*'s race around South America in 1898 helped galvanize American public opinion on the need for an American interocean canal. Thereafter, the design of the proposed American canal became closely intertwined with developments within the U.S. Navy. As larger American battleships were being designed, the width and depth of the projected canal channel and locks had to be constantly reappraised. The final determination came in January 1908 after the General Board of the U.S. Navy, in a memorandum to the secretary of the navy dated 29 October 1907, expressed its opinion that the planned canal lock width at Panama be increased from 100 feet to 110 feet. Seven months after the canal was opened, the battleship USS *Pennsylvania*, with a beam measurement of 97 feet 1 inch, was launched at Newport News, Virginia. Five years later, two battlecruisers, which eventually became America's first large aircraft carriers, were laid down with beam measurements of 106 feet. Even before these ships were launched, the 1918-built British battlecruiser HMS *Hood*, with a beam of 105 feet 2 inches, transited the canal without incident. The new interocean waterway could accommodate the extreme measurements of the new naval vessels, but with only inches to spare.

Sailing ships anchored in Gatun Lake provide a backdrop as HMS *Renown*, with the Prince of Wales aboard, and HMS *Calcutta* transit southbound on 30 March 1920. (National Archives)

In handling large fleet movements, the canal was first able to exhibit its proficiency during July 1919 when 33 vessels of the U.S. Pacific Fleet transited the isthmus, 30 of them in two days. Included in this armada were the twin 32,000-ton dreadnoughts, USS *New Mexico* and USS *Mississippi*, each 624 feet long with a beam measurement of 97 feet 4 inches. Twenty-two escorting destroyers, with an average length of 314 feet and an average beam of 31 feet, were handled through the 1,000-foot by 110-foot lock chambers six ships at a time. In later years the U.S. Navy would send larger fleets through Panama, all to be processed without mishap or unwarranted delay.

Visits by foreign naval vessels were to be less frequent. In the 1920s, Japan and Germany began sending cadet training vessels through the canal, usually obsolete warships that gave little indication of each country's growing military power. Great Britain maintained a warship at Bermuda on its North America and West Indies Station, and the vessel could be expected to transit the canal at least once or twice each year on goodwill voyages to the west coasts of North and South America. Other navies made irregular visits. In early 1921 the Chilean battleship *Almirante Latorre* transited in company with the destroyers *Riveros*, *Uribe*, and *Williams*. In July of that same year, while on a voyage between France and Peru, the French cruiser *Jules Michelet* collided with the bank at Gamboa and had to be placed in the Balboa dry dock for repairs. Three months later, the Italian cruiser *Libra* paid a courtesy call to Panama, docking at Balboa's Pier 18.

Red Hallen's camera captured many of these vessels. In his surviving photographs we are able to watch the development of America's battleships and witness the enormity of its first great aircraft carriers. We can also observe life as it was practiced six decades ago in several of the world's navies. The sharpness of Hallen's glass plates allows us to peer in among the transiting crews to glimpse their expressions, mannerisms, and dress. From views of transports and hospital ships returning from World War I to the haunting scenes of vessels that were to perish in the opening salvos of World War II, Hallen managed to record naval might and navy life as it existed when the battleship still ruled supreme, and air power had yet to make its mark on the oceans of the globe.

USS *Severn*

Before the Panama Canal became fully operational in August of 1914, several of the finished locks were used as dry docks for routine maintenance on various canal and navy vessels. In March and April 1914 one of the east chambers of Gatun Locks was used for this purpose. The U.S. Navy submarines C-1, C-2, C-3, C-4, and C-5, and the canal ladder dredge *Corozal* were dry-docked there for overhaul. At the same time, the submarine tender *Severn* was anchored above the lock in the fresh waters of Gatun Lake to kill off her barnacles. On April 11th the five submarines and the dredge were refloated. The dredge was to return to its work in Culebra Cut, while the five submarines joined the *Severn* for maneuvers and testing on the lake. Four days later the six naval craft returned to the Atlantic, stepping down through the locks on April 15th. This photograph shows the *Severn* being handled out of the upper east chamber at Gatun by four electric "mules," with the five submarines waiting at the far end of the chamber. As this was one of the first transit operations through Gatun, a number of spectators were present for the occasion. The *Severn* had been built in 1898 as the three-masted bark *Chesapeake* for use by midshipmen of the U.S. Naval Academy at Annapolis. In 1910 the wooden-sheathed vessel was refitted as a submarine tender and three years later was sent south to Panama. In 1916 the ship was returned to Norfolk, Virginia, under tow and sold out of the navy.

28

Presidente Sarmiento

The canal was new and the grass freshly planted along Miraflores Lock when the Argentine training ship *Presidente Sarmiento* transited from the Pacific to the Atlantic on 14 July 1915. Named after President Domingo Faustino Sarmiento, founder of the Argentine Naval Academy, the *Presidente Sarmiento* had been built by Cammell Laird, Birkenhead, in 1897 to a design that resembled the "fifty-fifty" naval corvettes of the nineteenth century. In these ships both steam and sail could be used to provide power on an equal basis. The *Presidente Sarmiento* was both ship-rigged and steam-powered, her compound engines developing 2,800 indicated horsepower and giving 15 knots. The vessel's two slender funnels can be seen amidships. Her bunker capacity of 330 tons of coal provided for a steaming range of approximately 4,500 miles at an average speed of 10 knots. An interesting feature of her design is the stern-walk, a balcony-like structure wrapped around the stern of the vessel just below the poop. Three sailors are making use of the stern-walk in this picture, watching as water fills the lock to lift their vessel to the level of Miraflores Lake. At sea, and in calm weather, the stern-walk might be covered with an awning to give officers aboard some seclusion. The 2,850-ton displacement *Presidente Sarmiento* made 37 deep-sea training cruises during her life span, covering over one million nautical miles. Her last training voyage was made in 1939, and she was finally decommissioned in 1961. Today, she remains afloat as a stationary museum ship in Argentina.

USS *Ohio*

Several crewmen perched on her aft cage mast receive a good dose of coal smoke as the 1901-built American predreadnought battleship *Ohio* transits Panama on 16 July 1915 during a summer training cruise. With a 72-foot beam, the widest of any ship to have transited the canal to that date, the *Ohio* was placed under tow while passing Cucaracha Slide. Armed for broadsides, the warship carried four 12-inch guns in two turrets and sixteen 6-inch guns. Though not gloried in combat during her 22-year lifespan, the *Ohio* still received her share of publicity. In 1905, as flagship of the U.S. Asiatic Fleet, the 12,723-ton vessel embarked the party of William Howard Taft, then secretary of war, at Manila for a Far Eastern tour of inspection. Included in this distinguished group was Miss Alice Roosevelt, the president's daughter. Two years later, the *Ohio* was included in a fleet of sixteen predreadnought battleships that were sent off around the world by President Roosevelt to show both the American flag and American might. The cruise of the "Great White Fleet" did very much what the president had hoped it would, leaving behind a somewhat calmer world, particularly in the Far East. When newer battleships eventually displaced the *Ohio* from front-line service, the elderly vessel was pressed into training work, employment that saw her through World War I. Finally placed in reserve during early 1919, the veteran navy unit was decommissioned on 31 May 1922 and sold for scrap one year later.

USS *Charleston*

Photographed in the recently completed dry dock at Balboa, the protected U.S. cruiser *Charleston* steams placidly, as a small group of her crew appear to be analyzing the alignment of her keel. It is 8 September 1916, and America's entry into World War I is imminent. Launched by Newport News Shipbuilding and Dry Dock Co. in 1904, the 9,700-ton displacement *Charleston* saw duty in many areas of the world. Her first visit to Panama occurred in the summer of 1906 when she disembarked Secretary of State Elihu Root and party following a goodwill mission to Latin America. Two years later, the *Charleston* was sent to the Far East, where she later became flagship of the U.S. Asiatic Fleet based in the Philippines. In May of 1916 the cruiser was transferred to Panama to act as tender for U.S. submarines in the area. She performed this duty until the United States entered World War I, at which time the ship sailed for St. Thomas in the Virgin Islands to join other units of the U.S. fleet. After the war, the *Charleston* made several expeditions to Europe, ferrying occupation troops eastbound and returning with combat veterans. The warship's last post was at San Diego, California, where she acted as administrative flagship for Commander, Destroyer Squadrons, Pacific Fleet until 1923. In June of that year, the vessel steamed for Puget Sound, where she was decommissioned on December 4th. Seven years later the ship was sold for scrap.

Cartagena

On 22 November 1917, an old adversary was photographed at the Cristóbal coaling docks. The 1,200-ton-displacement Colombian gunboat *Cartagena*, looking very much the worse for wear, was berthed alongside. The warship had originally been built in 1892 by "Orlando," Leghorn, Italy, as the *El Baschir* for the government of Morocco. Sold to Colombia in 1902, the small vessel sailed across the Atlantic just in time to become embroiled in the Panamanian revolution. On the evening of 2 November 1903, the warship, now renamed *Cartagena*, brought a contingent of approximately 500 Colombian troops to Colón to reinforce the local garrison. (At that time, Panama was still part of Colombia.) Also in the harbor lay the American gunboat, USS *Nashville*, which had arrived only a few hours earlier to watch over American interests in the area. Unknown to the commanders of both the *Nashville* and *Cartagena*, a revolutionary movement was at that time already under way in Panama City. Only by quick action, hard negotiation, and the payment of a considerable amount of money, were the Colombian troops and their commanders finally persuaded to depart the isthmus peacefully. Their exit, however, had to be on the British-owned Royal Mail liner SS *Orinoco*, because the *Cartagena*, well-outgunned by the *Nashville*, had already steamed back over the horizon. The chastened Colombian gunboat lived on to serve as a patrol vessel in the Caribbean through World War I, but was reported to have been placed out of service by 1924.

USS *Tallahassee*

A familiar visitor to the U.S. Naval Academy at Annapolis after the turn of the century, the 1901-built *Tallahassee* is shown in the large 1,000-foot by 110-foot dry dock at Balboa during World War I. As the dock is being emptied of water in preparation for dry-docking, members of the crew can be seen at their leisure, one sailor perched on the foremast with a good book in hand. The *Tallahassee*, built as a coastal monitor, had been moved to Panama in 1917 to tend submarines in the area, duty for which she had earlier been modified at Norfolk, Virginia. Launched as the *Florida* by the Crescent Shipyard, Elizabethport, N.J., the ship's name was changed to *Tallahassee* in 1908, her original designation going over to U.S. Battleship No. 30, then under construction. It was as the *Florida*, however, that the monitor regularly sailed from Annapolis each summer with midshipmen aboard. This duty was interrupted in early 1907 for gunnery-testing purposes. Worried about the possible effect on gun crews of a second turret firing directly over a lower turret, as would be practiced in later battleships, the navy fired several 12-inch gun blasts over the *Tallahassee*'s own manned turret. The test demonstrated that gun crews were adequately protected. Four years later the monitor was used to test high-explosive shells on the hulk of the old battleship *Texas* in Chesapeake Bay. At the end of her own career in 1922, the *Tallahassee* was sold to the Ammunition Products Corporation, Washington, D.C. for use as scrap.

Marama

On 22 April 1918, after transiting the canal on a voyage from Avonmouth to Auckland, the New Zealand hospital ship *Marama* docked at Balboa's Pier 18. Aboard were a large number of wounded soldiers being returned home from European battlefields. The stop at Balboa was short, only long enough for food and water to be taken on board. The following morning the floating hospital and her weary load resumed the long journey across the Pacific, reaching Auckland on May 14th. The *Marama* had been built by Caird & Co. Ltd., Greenock, in 1907 as a coal-burning passenger ship for the Union Steamship Company of New Zealand. A small liner of 6,437-tons, the vessel could accommodate 229 first-class, 79 second-class, and 153 third-class passengers. For a number of years the *Marama* was employed in transpacific service between New Zealand and San Francisco, but this duty was cut short in 1914 when the ship was requisitioned by the New Zealand government for war work. Converted into a hospital ship at Port Chalmers, the liner made eight voyages to and from the United Kingdom carrying wounded during the conflict. After her war duty, the *Marama* returned to the Pacific passenger trade. Sold in 1937, she made her final departure from New Zealand on August 10 of that year en route to Shanghai, China. In early 1938 the 30-year-old ship was resold to Myochi Kisen KK, of Kobe, Japan. The liner was broken up for scrap at Osaka just a few months before war again broke out in Europe.

Comfort

The American hospital ship *Comfort* was the first vessel to pass through the Panama Canal with wounded Americans from World War I. The appearance of the white-hulled mercy ship at Pedro Miguel Locks on 19 June 1919 brought a number of spectators to the site. Questions and answers regarding the war were exchanged between visitors and passengers as the *Comfort* paused while transiting between Charleston, South Carolina, and San Francisco Bay. The *Comfort* had been built in 1907 as the passenger vessel *Havana* by Wm. Cramp & Sons, Philadelphia, for the Ward Line. At the start of World War I, the liner was taken over by the War Department for use as an army transport, the USAT *Havana*, but was transferred to the navy on 17 July 1917 for duty as a hospital ship. After being commissioned on 18 March 1918, the *Comfort* became a floating hospital for several months at New York, then joined the Cruiser and Transport Force, Atlantic Fleet to return war wounded from Europe. In three voyages undertaken between 21 October 1918 and 13 March 1919, the *Comfort* brought 1,183 men home from France, Britain, and the Azores. Following the transit shown here, the ship was decommissioned at Mare Island Navy Yard in 1921 and re-entered commercial service as the *Havana* four years later. During the early 1940s, the liner again took up wartime duties, first serving as the army transport *Aguileon* and later as the army hospital ship *Shamrock*. A year after being redelivered to the War Shipping Administration in 1946, the vessel was sold for scrap.

USS *Texas*

The first passage of a large U.S. naval fleet through the Panama Canal took place in July 1919, when a total of 33 vessels transited from the Atlantic to the Pacific. It was the type of work the canal had been built for, and all systems lived up to expectations. The battleship *Texas*, one of the faster vessels, accomplished its transit in 10 hours, 28 minutes, discounting 21 hours and 5 minutes spent at anchor in Gatun Lake. The passage of the fleet challenged the canal's stores and fueling facilities. A total of 13,000 tons of coal and 48,233 barrels of oil were furnished to the ships during their visit. Food items supplied to the vessels ranged from 52,391 pounds of beef and 7,604 dozen eggs to 531 pounds of sauerkraut and 706 quarts of ice cream. In the course of the navy's visit, Panama City received its first large-scale invasion by free-spending U.S. sailors, and shopowners forever after looked forward to their return. Unique to the *Texas* on this transit was an airplane, seen here poised like a small soapbox racer on the warship's upper forward turret. Four months earlier the French-built Hanriot HD-1 had been flown off the gun mount by Lieutenant Commander Edward O. McDonnell, thus bringing aviation to the U.S. battleship fleet. Following strenuous service in World War II, the *Texas* made her final transit of the canal in 1946 en route to Norfolk, Virginia. On 21 April 1948 the by then much-modified battleship was decommissioned at San Jacinto State Park where she still rests as a permanent memorial.

USS *Vermont*

On her way from the Atlantic to the Pacific, the 1905-built U.S. battleship *Vermont* is shown in the upper west chamber of Gatun Locks. The 16,000-ton warship made only three transits of the Panama Canal in her lifetime. The most publicized of these was her voyage south to Chile in June 1918 with the body of the late Chilean ambassador to the United States aboard. The body was escorted by the U.S. ambassador to Chile, the Honorable J.H. Shea, who disembarked at Valparaiso before the battleship returned to the United States in early July. The third and final transit was the one pictured here, a journey in the summer of 1919 that carried the *Vermont* and her crew from Hampton Roads, Virginia, to San Francisco Bay. After transiting the canal on July 25th, the warship proceeded up the Pacific coast for visits to San Diego, San Pedro, Monterey, and Astoria before tying up at Mare Island on September 18th. The *Vermont* was decommissioned there on 30 June 1920 and, in accordance with the Washington Treaty limiting naval armament, sold for scrap three years later. In the opposite lock and slightly behind the battleship is the Blue Star Line cargo vessel *Camana*, bound from Liverpool to Point Napier, New Zealand. Built by Dunlop, Bremner & Co. in 1918 and later renamed *Celtic Star*, the 5,575-ton British freighter was lost in the Atlantic on 30 March 1943, the victim of an Italian submarine. Two men were killed and another taken prisoner in the incident.

USS *Nebraska*

On 31 July 1919 the battleship USS *Nebraska* transited the canal on its way to the Pacific coast. Laid down at Seattle, Washington, during 1902 and launched in 1904, the *Nebraska* had been a member of Roosevelt's "Great White Fleet," which she joined at San Francisco in May 1908. Her epic round-the-world voyage was followed by an appearance at the Hudson-Fulton Celebration in 1910 and at the Louisiana Centennial during 1912. Though heavily armed with four 12-inch guns and eight 8-inch guns, the *Nebraska* spent most of World War I acting as a training ship and transport. Following four transatlantic voyages, during which she carried a total of 4,540 soldiers, the battleship was transferred to Division 2, Squadron 1, of the U.S. Pacific Fleet. Photographed in the east chamber of Pedro Miguel Lock during her Panama transit, the *Nebraska* is shown with most of her crew on deck. A few men have climbed to the top of the mainmast and foremast for a better view. The lattice-style masts were designed to limit damage by shell fire, but in practice proved easily susceptible to corrosion. Anti-shrapnel mattresses are seen tied to railings and masts. Of interest are the battleship's superposed turrets incorporating two 12-inch guns and twin 8-inch guns, a configuration later dropped in U.S. battleship design. After operating along the Pacific coast for a year, the *Nebraska* was decommissioned on 2 July 1920, and in accordance with the Washington Treaty limiting naval armament, sold for scrap in late 1923.

U.S. Destroyers *Schley, Badger,* and *Hazelwood*

On 28 August 1919 the U.S. destroyers *Schley* (DD 103), *Badger* (DD 126), and *Hazelwood* (DD 107) transited Panama while on a voyage from New York to San Diego. All three vessels were returning from postwar duties in the Mediterranean area. Though built within months of each other, the ships went on to lead quite separate lives. The *Hazelwood* was decommissioned within three years of arriving in California. Recommissioned in 1925 for training missions, the destroyer was again taken out of service in 1930 and sold for scrap in 1935. The *Badger* decommissioned in 1922, but recommissioned in 1930 and transferred to the Atlantic three years later. When World War II broke out, the vessel was pressed into convoy escort duty, employment that kept her occupied for the next three years. In late 1944 the ship again visited Panama on an antisubmarine exercise and remained in the Caribbean area for an additional year with the U.S. Antisubmarine Development Detachment. In July 1945 the *Badger* was finally decommissioned at Philadelphia and within three months of war's end sold for scrap. The *Schley*, though placed out of commission for 18 years, was reactivated in 1940 and sent to Hawaii, where she survived the 7 December 1941 attack on Pearl Harbor. For the next year the ship was used for patrol work. In early 1943 the *Schley* was converted into a fast transport and reclassified APD 14. In this role the warship took part in a number of strategic island invasions. Worn out by 1945, the veteran combat vessel was broken up at the Philadelphia Navy Yard in 1946. A fourth ship of the same class, unidentified, is nearly obscured by the first pair.

USAT *Mt. Vernon*

Bright sunlight highlights the USAT *Mount Vernon* and assisting tug *Mariner* as they ease past dredges near Cucaracha Slide on 25 May 1920. The U.S. Army transport had originally been built in 1906 as the passenger liner *Kronprinzessin Cecilie* for North German Lloyd, but in 1917 the 19,505-ton ship was seized at Boston by the United States government and handed over to the U.S. Navy for military duty as the *Mount Vernon*. Following strenuous service in World War I, during which the liner made nine Atlantic crossings and was damaged by a torpedo fired from German submarine U-82, she was transferred to the U.S. War Department for service as an army repatriation ship. Her first sailing in this new employment was from New York to Vladivostok, Russia, in the fall of 1919. She is pictured here during the return from that voyage with 3,220 Czechoslovak soldiers, 294 Czechoslovak and French officers and dependents, and 698 German prisoners aboard, all for repatriation to Europe. The *Mount Vernon* had left the Russian port on 13 April 1920 and reached Balboa on May 24th by way of San Francisco. After loading over 6,000 tons of coal at canal coaling stations and having her refrigeration machinery repaired, the *Mount Vernon* sailed for Hamburg on June 5th. Equipped with the largest steam reciprocating machinery ever built into a merchant vessel, the *Mount Vernon* consumed an average of 375 tons of coal a day on her round-trip journey, a trip made at an average speed of 13.5 knots. The *Mount Vernon* was laid up in Chesapeake Bay during 1924 and sold for scrap 16 years later.

USS *Michigan*

Launched in 1908, the USS *Michigan*, along with the USS *South Carolina*, was the first of America's dreadnought battleships. As such, she mounted eight 12-inch guns along with 22 3-inch guns and had a speed of 18.5 knots. Her construction was the result of considerable effort by President Theodore Roosevelt to build a modern U.S. Navy capable of facing Japan's growing naval strength in the Pacific. The *Michigan* saw service along the coast of Mexico in 1913 and 1914, then operated as a transport in 1919, bringing 1,052 American soldiers home from World War I. In the summer of 1920 the battleship made a training cruise from Annapolis to Hawaii with several hundred midshipmen aboard. This 13 June 1920 photograph shows the *Michigan* being followed through the canal by the *South Carolina* and two escorting tugs. Serpent-like canvas ventilators arc from the vessel's superstructure to catch air for crews working below. On the canal bank, in the foreground of this picture, two men watch the warship pass by. The 12-year old *Michigan* was already near the end of her operational lifespan. Though of a pioneering design for the U.S. Navy, the 16,000-ton-displacement warship had been rendered obsolete by newer construction. After returning from her 1920 training cruise to Hawaii, the *Michigan* undertook a second training cruise to Europe in the summer of 1921. This was the vessel's last voyage. She was decommissioned at Philadelphia in February 1922 and broken up for scrap two years later.

USS *Arizona*

On 23 February 1921 one of America's "super-dreadnoughts," the battleship USS *Arizona*, passed through the canal on a transit from Balboa to Guantánamo Bay, Cuba. In this picture, taken from one of the floating cranes at Paraiso, a group of sailors can be seen on deck cleaning and securing equipment for sea. The warship's main armor belt, eighteen feet wide and fourteen inches thick, is distinctly visible along the hull. Fifty-four vessels of the Atlantic Fleet, composed of seven battleships, eighteen destroyers, and twenty-nine smaller vessels, had transited the canal southbound one month earlier. At Balboa the major units joined with elements of the U.S. Pacific Fleet—eight battleships and sixteen destroyers—for a training cruise along the west coast of South America. On return to Panama in mid-February, the two fleets rested at Balboa for a week, during which time shore leave was granted for over 20,000 men daily. President Belisario Porras of Panama entertained U.S. officers, while enlisted men took in bullfights and baseball games. Before the big ships weighed anchor, over a million dollars had been deposited in the local economy. The 1915-built *Arizona*, armed with four turrets of 14-inch guns and twenty-two 5-inch guns, was one of the most heavily armed and armored vessels of her time. Her heavy protection, however, proved useless on 7 December 1941; a Japanese surprise attack completely destroyed the battleship in minutes, leaving the *Arizona* submerged at Pearl Harbor, where she remains today as a permanent memorial.

Izumo

With coal smoke billowing from her funnels and midshipmen lined up at every vantage point, the 9,750-ton Japanese cruiser *Izumo* moves out of Miraflores Locks on 15 October 1921. The British-built *Izumo* was on a round-the-world training voyage in company with the smaller, German-built Japanese cruiser *Yakumo*. Both ships were under the command of Vice Admiral Saito. They had arrived at Balboa from San Diego on October 9th. During their six-day stay at Panama, the Japanese midshipmen were given an extensive tour of canal facilities, which included visits to Miraflores Locks and the port terminals of Cristóbal and Balboa. The training squadron then cleared for New York. Designed by Philip Watts and built in 1899 by Armstrong, Whitworth & Company, Elswick, the *Izumo* had been the flagship of Admiral Kamimura at the Battle of Tsushima during the Russo-Japanese War and had accounted for herself well in that engagement. In later years the *Izumo* was re-rated as a coast-defense ship. The vessel made a number of annual training voyages in this role, transiting the Panama Canal with the *Asama* and *Iwate* under the overall command of Vice Admiral Tanaguchi in 1922, and with *Asama* and *Yakumo* under the overall command of Vice Admiral Saburo Hyakutake in 1924. As tensions rose in the Far East, the *Izumo* was made the flagship of the Japanese China Fleet in 1932 and again became a 1st-Class cruiser in 1942. On 28 July 1945, while being used as a training vessel at Kure, the veteran warship was attacked by U.S. aircraft and destroyed. The hulk was broken up at Harima in 1947.

HMS *Raleigh*

On 18 February 1922, the new British cruiser HMS *Raleigh* passed through the canal with Vice Admiral Sir William Pakenham on board. As flagship of the Royal Navy's North America and West Indies Squadron, the ship was returning from a three-month cruise along the Pacific coasts of the United States and Canada. This view, taken from Gatun Lighthouse, shows the vessel centered in the upper west chamber of Gatun Locks with the chamber gates about to close. Because of the tropical climate, the *Raleigh* has considerable canvas spread to provide deck shelter. A large number of her crew wear pith helmets as an additional protection against the heat. To the left side of the picture, beyond the cruiser, is the small settlement of Gatun and its fenced tennis courts. Note the cluster of vehicles nearby. The *Raleigh* had previously passed through Panama on 23 November 1921, en route to San Diego from Jamaica, and had fueled at Cristóbal. Laid down during World War I, the 9,750-ton *Raleigh* was not finished until 1921. Following her visit to Panama, the warship continued on to Bermuda and from there, sailed for Montreal, Canada, during the summer of 1922. While returning from the Canadian port to Bermuda on 8 August 1922, the 30-knot vessel ran aground in thick fog off Point Armour, Labrador, and became a total loss. Ten members of the ship's crew perished in the incident. The rest managed to reach shore safely and were picked up by the Canadian Pacific liner *Montrose*. The wreck of the *Raleigh* was later sold to J. Tardiff of Montreal for dismantling.

Iwate

In the summer of 1922, the Japanese cruiser *Iwate*, in company with the *Asama* and *Izumo*, transited Panama from the Pacific to the Atlantic on a training voyage to Brazil. The 9,750-ton *Iwate* is seen passing Cucaracha Slide, with many of her crew out on deck. All three Japanese ships were under the command of Vice Admiral Tanaguchi and had a total of 2,412 men on board. The *Iwate* had been built in Great Britain at the turn of the century and along with the *Asama* and *Iwate*, had performed with valor at the historic battle of Tsushima in 1905. Although they were obsolete by the 1920s, the constant appearance of the Tsushima survivors at western ports may have served to wrongly influence U.S. public opinion as to the threat of Japanese sea power at the time. During its 1922 cruise, the training squadron stayed at Cristóbal for three days and then cleared for Rio de Janeiro, where the ships and their company were to take part in a centennial exposition. The Japanese cruisers paid approximately $5,000 each in transit fees and took on several hundred tons of coal and provisions while at Panama. Their well-behaved crews were welcomed ashore, although they reportedly spent far less money than their American counterparts. By the late 1930s, mounting tensions in the Pacific put an end to the trans-Panama training voyages. In 1942 the *Iwate* was again rated as a 1st-Class cruiser. The aged warship was sunk by U.S. aircraft at Kure just a few weeks before World War II came to a close.

USS *Utah*

An American man-of-war, the battleship *Utah* cruises past Gold Hill and the spent rubble of Cucaracha Slide on 15 February 1923. The warship was on its way to Balboa to join in maneuvers with the Pacific Fleet. Eighty-eight vessels of the United States Navy, comprising a major portion of the Atlantic Fleet, crossed the isthmus between February 1st and 17th. Included in the movement were seven battleships, two cruisers, twenty destroyers, and twenty-seven submarines. The *Utah*, launched in 1909, was one of twelve American battleships completed to dreadnought design in a ten-year building program pushed through in its early stages by President Theodore Roosevelt. The warship displaced 21,825 tons and mounted ten 12-inch guns in five turrets as main armament. By the time the final ships of the series, the *Pennsylvania* and *Arizona*, were completed in 1915/16, displacement tonnage was up to 31,400, and twelve 14-inch guns were being carried in four turrets. The *Utah* led a highly interesting career that included service off Mexico in 1914 and operation in European waters during World War I. In 1931 the battleship was converted into a mobile target vessel (AG 16) at the Norfolk Navy Yard and for the next decade assisted in the training of gun crews and bombardiers. On 7 December 1941, while moored at Pearl Harbor, the ship became a target for Japanese aviators and was sunk during the first few minutes of the surprise attack, with the loss of 64 men. The submerged hulk remains at the navy base today.

64

U.S. Grant

On 7 May 1923 the United States Army transport *U.S. Grant* passed through the canal on a voyage from New York to San Francisco. The white-hulled transport had a contingent of U.S. soldiers aboard as well as 2,200 tons of military stores. The weather was excellent, and all troops were out on deck. In the foreground, just beyond the lock gate, two women can be seen sharing a single parasol against the incessant tropical sun. Nearer the ship a group of gentlemen and officers take in transit procedures. The transport has been stepped up through the three west chambers of Gatun Locks and is now about to enter Gatun Lake. In the adjacent lock a small black-hulled ship is visible through lamp posts lining the east chamber. This is the 4,466-ton passenger-cargo vessel *Ucayali* of the Peruvian Line. The *Ucayali*, with 646 tons of cargo on board, was proceeding from Cristóbal to Guayaquil. On 6 July 1923, the *U.S. Grant* again transited the canal on a return voyage from the Pacific coast to New York, a service she completed at regular intervals. The American transport had been built in 1907 as the German liner *Konig Wilhelm II*, but was taken over by the United States government during World War I and renamed *Madawaska*. After a lengthy refit in 1922, the ship was rechristened *U.S. Grant*. Following service with the army, the ex-liner was transferred to the U.S. Navy in 1941 and used as a military transport throughout World War II. After being returned to the army in 1946, the vessel was sold for scrap during 1947.

Jeanne D'Arc

With her crew in pith helmets to shield them from the tropical sun, the French cruiser *Jeanne D'Arc* steams southbound through Gaillard Cut on 2 December 1923. Under the command of Captain Bourdoncle de Saint Salvy, the warship had been sent to Panama by the French government in connection with the unveiling of a monument at Panama City. The vessel reached Cristóbal on November 30th and attracted considerable attention because of her novel profile. Built as the French Navy's first large armored cruiser, the *Jeanne D'Arc* was laid down in October 1896 but not completed until 1902. Each of her six funnels, laid out in two separated groups of three, served a single boiler room containing six boilers. Although the 36 boilers were to give 33,000 ihp, producing 23 knots, the ship did not live up to her designers' expectations. Because of this, the vessel was most often used in a training role, with most of her armament landed. After transiting the canal, the *Jeanne D'Arc* docked at Balboa, allowing Captain Bourdoncle de Saint Salvy to attend dedication ceremonies in Panama City on December 4th. The French captain and several of his officers then went on to place a wreath at the foot of a tablet commemorating canal company employees who had lost their lives in World War I. Following these ceremonies, the *Jeanne D'Arc* departed Balboa on December 6th for San Francisco. Less than a decade later the aged cruiser was withdrawn from service and sold for scrap.

USS *Pennsylvania*

While existing only on paper during the construction of the Panama Canal, the 31,400-ton-displacement *Pennsylvania*-class battleship played a major role in the final design of the waterway. Because of the ship's wide beam of 97 feet 1 inch, the navy requested that the canal locks, yet to be constructed, be increased to a width of 110 feet from the 95 feet planned. The request was granted, and thus the *Pennsylvania* class set the standards to which the Panama Canal locks were eventually completed. On the transit photographed here, the *Pennsylvania* was proceeding to the Caribbean on 24 March 1924 for maneuvers. Degree marks visible on the battleship's turrets were intended to give other vessels in the battleline the *Pennsylvania*'s target bearing, while the circular dial on the cage mast signaled target range. Dispatched to the Hawaiian Islands in 1941, the *Pennsylvania* was caught in dry dock on December 7th. One of the first vessels to respond to the Japanese air attack, the battleship was hit several times and damaged. Once repaired, however, the *Pennsylvania* made up for lost time, earning a total of eight battle stars. A few days before hostilities ceased, a single Japanese plane managed to evade defenses at Okinawa and torpedo the vessel as she lay at anchor. The resulting explosion killed twenty men and injured ten others. Patched up at Guam, the ship steamed for Puget Sound, Washington, losing a propeller and shaft along the way. In July 1946 the combat veteran was used as a target vessel for nuclear detonations at Bikini Atoll. After tests on her hull were completed in 1948, the *Pennsylvania* was unceremoniously sunk in deep water.

USS *Neches*

While the latest and largest battleships claimed most of the attention at Panama, smaller naval units were occasionally caught by the camera. One such ship was the fleet tanker USS *Neches* (AO 5), photographed while transiting on 5 April 1924. Originally launched by the Boston Navy Yard in 1920 as Fuel Ship No. 17, the *Neches* was to handle various duties in her lifetime. These ranged from mail and stores delivery to towing gunnery targets. When fleet exercises were to be carried out in the Bay of Panama, the *Neches* would typically arrive before the main battle units, carrying up to 53,000 barrels of fuel oil for the ships. Later stationed at San Diego, the *Neches* was halfway between that port and Honolulu, Hawaii, with a full load of fuel on board when word was received of the 7 December 1941 attack on Pearl Harbor. The tanker proceeded to her destination, arriving at Pearl Harbor on December 10th. After discharge and a quick return voyage to San Diego for additional oil, the *Neches* again steamed out of Pearl Harbor late in the afternoon of 22 January 1942, bound for the western Pacific. Shortly after midnight a submarine contact was made. While attempting to evade the intruder, later identified as Japanese submarine I-172, the *Neches* was hit by what was thought to be a "dud" torpedo. Nine minutes later a second torpedo hit, this time exploding near the ship's engine room. A third explosion followed, after which the *Neches* settled quickly, sinking at 4:37 A.M. with the loss of fifty-seven of her crew.

HMS *Repulse*

In 1923/24 the British government sent a squadron of its most powerful warships around the globe on a goodwill mission. Known as the British Special Service Squadron, the ships sailed from London on 27 October 1923 and reach Panama by way of the Cape of Good Hope on 23 July 1924. The capital units of this fleet were the battlecruisers HMS *Hood* and HMS *Repulse*. Four light cruisers attached to the squadron continued south from Panama to the Strait of Magellan, while the *Hood* and *Repulse*, followed by the Australian cruiser *Adelaide*, transited the isthmus for Jamaica. The *Repulse,* shown passing through Gaillard Cut on July 24th, was a sister to the battlecruiser *Renown*, which had first transited Panama on a voyage to New Zealand in 1920. Completed in June of 1916 by John Brown & Company, Clydebank, the *Repulse* was 794 feet 2 inches in length, with a beam of 102 feet 8 inches and a standard displacement of 32,000 tons. Her loaded displacement at the time of this transit was 35,359 tons, requiring tolls of $17,679.50 to be paid. Though a powerful-looking ship, the *Repulse* was lightly armored. On 10 December 1941, while in company with the new British battleship *Prince of Wales*, the *Repulse* was attacked by a large number of Japanese warplanes off the east coast of Malaya. The ship was hit by a bomb that penetrated through to her engine room. During a second attack by torpedo-carrying aircraft, the battlecruiser was again hit and mortally wounded. The *Repulse* sank with a loss of 434 men; the sinking of the *Prince of Wales* followed later that same day.

74

HMS *Hood*

On 24 July 1924 the British battlecruiser HMS *Hood* transited Panama as part of the British Special Service Squadron, which was making a round-the-world voyage. At the time of her transit, HMS *Hood* was the largest man-of-war in existence, and her passage across Panama set new canal records for vessel length, beam, displacement, and tolls paid. Laid down by John Brown, Clydebank, in 1916 and completed in 1920, the *Hood* measured 860 feet 7 inches in length and 105 feet 2.5 inches in beam. This gave the warship a clearance of 2 feet 4.75 inches on either side and 70 feet fore and aft in the 110-foot by 1,000-foot canal locks. The battlecruiser's greatest beam, its protective armor belt, lay below the waterline. To give the canal pilot aboard a better indication of clearances, several outrigger poles were attached to the vessel. Seamen were stationed at these poles to signal with flags if the ship should approach closer than 2 feet to the lock wall. Centering control was provided by eight canal towing locomotives, four positioned on each side of the vessel. All three warships were handled through the locks without incident, although the *Hood* and *Repulse* were tied up for the night of July 23rd at Pedro Miguel. This photograph shows the *Hood* passing the La Pita Point Improvement Project on the following morning. The 44,799-ton-displacement warship paid a record toll of $22,399.50 for her transit. Seventeen years later the *Hood* was sunk by the German battleship *Bismarck*. She went down within minutes of exploding, with the loss of all but three of her crew.

USS *Langley*

To viewers along the canal on 16 November 1924, this strange transiting vessel must have seemed a very unlikely warship, yet what they were witnessing was the dawn of a new age in naval warfare—the age of the aircraft carrier. The USS *Langley*, the first aircraft carrier in the United States Navy, had originally been completed as a 19,360-ton collier, the *Jupiter* (AC 3), but was transformed into a "flattop" during the early 1920s. Even in her original guise, however, the ship had been revolutionary and, in fact, historic as far as the Panama Canal was concerned. Not only was the *Jupiter* the first U.S. Navy vessel to be electrically propelled, it was also the first U.S. Navy vessel to transit the Panama Canal, an undertaking accomplished on 10 October 1914. On the particular transit shown here, the *Langley* was en route from Norfolk, Virginia, to San Diego, California, to join the Pacific Battle Fleet. After duty in the Pacific training pilots for the navy's next two carriers, the *Lexington* and *Saratoga*, the *Langley* was again converted, this time into a seaplane tender at Mare Island, California. Pressed into emergency service as an aircraft transport during the early days of WW II, the ship was spotted and bombed by Japanese aircraft south of Java on 27 February 1942. Severely damaged, the burning vessel and her cargo of 32 P-40 fighter planes had to be destroyed by the escorting destroyers *Whipple* and *Edsall* later that same day.

Hamburg

Like Japan, Germany regularly sent a unit of its naval fleet on a global training cruise. The first of these vessels to pass through the Panama Canal, the light cruiser *Berlin*, arrived at Cristóbal on 30 October 1925 with 80 midshipmen on board. The ship paid tolls amounting to $1,853.50 for her transit from Port-au-Prince to Guayaquil on November 2nd. She was followed in April of 1926 by the cruiser *Hamburg*, photographed here in Miraflores Locks. As with most transits involving training ships, a local cameraman has come out from Panama City to take souvenir photographs of the crew. He is using a camera similar to that used by the canal's official photographer. In the following year, the German Navy's midshipmen's cruise was undertaken by the *Emden*, which arrived at Balboa from Manzanillo, Mexico, on the afternoon of 6 September 1927. The 6,900-ton *Emden* did not transit the canal, but instead continued down the coast to Guayaquil, Ecuador. Launched in 1925, the *Emden* was Germany's first postwar cruiser, while the *Berlin* and *Hamburg* were war survivors from an earlier era. The *Hamburg* had been completed by the "Vulcan" shipyard, Stettin, in 1904, and the *Berlin* followed from Imperial Dockyard, Danzig, in 1905. In 1945 the *Emden* was scuttled in Heikendorf Bay after suffering extensive bomb damage. The 3,300-ton *Berlin* and *Hamburg*, both hulked in the 1930s, met similar fates. The *Berlin* was scuttled in 1947 with a load of poison gas aboard, while the *Hamburg*, sunk during the war, was refloated and broken up for scrap in 1949.

K-XIII

Panama Canal towing crews watch one of their smaller customers depart Pedro Miguel Locks on 28 July 1926. En route from Holland to the Dutch East Indies, the Dutch *K-XIII* became the first foreign submarine to transit Panama while in active service. The ship was on its maiden voyage and had left the Dutch Navy Base Den Helder at Nieuwediep on May 27th under the command of Lieutenant L.G.S. Van der Kun. The warship undertook goodwill calls at Horta, Las Palmas, and Curaçao before arriving at Cristóbal on the morning of July 24th. Following a four-day visit, the underwater vessel transited to Balboa on July 28th. Displacing 737 tons on the surface, the *K-XIII* paid $368.50 in canal tolls. Once in the Pacific, the submarine proceeded on to the Dutch East Indies via Mazatlán, San Francisco, Honolulu, Guam, Yap, Manila, and Amboina, arriving at Soerabaja on 13 December 1926. Four officers, 8 petty officers, and 18 sailors were on board for the six-and-a-half-month voyage. Although well armed with two 53.3-cm torpedo tubes, four 45-cm torpedo tubes, and an 8.8-cm deck gun, the *K-XIII* was unlucky in war. On 21 December 1941, while visiting Singapore, a battery explosion severely crippled the vessel. Taken to Soerabaja for repairs, the disabled Dutch submarine had to be destroyed by its own personnel on 2 March 1942 in the face of rapidly advancing Japanese forces.

HMS *Renown*

The British battlecruiser HMS *Renown* made a majestic sight on 25 January 1927 as she paused in Pedro Miguel Lock during a voyage from the United Kingdom to New Zealand and Australia. On board were the Duke and Duchess of York. The battle-cruiser had arrived at Cristóbal at 6 o'clock that morning and had been escorted into port by the U.S. battleship *Arkansas*, which had come down from Guantánamo, Cuba, for the occasion. The *Renown* made an immediate transit to Gatun, where the royal party disembarked for an inspection of the locks and spillway. The ship then continued on through the canal to dock at Balboa's Pier 6 late that afternoon. In the evening a reception was held in the newly completed British Legation in Panama City. On the following day the *Renown* cleared for the Marquesas Islands, where she was to be refueled by the British tanker *Delphinula*. The *Delphinula* had passed through Panama southbound on January 10th with 6,279 tons of fuel oil on board. This was the *Renown*'s third transit of the canal. The warship had passed through twice before with the Prince of Wales on board during a 1920 round-trip voyage to New Zealand. On the earlier transits, the *Renown*'s beam measurement had been 91 feet 6 inches and her displacement tonnage 33,379. On the transit photographed here, the vessel's beam measurement was 103 feet and her displacement tonnage up to 37,000, the result of added armor protection along and below the waterline. After valiant service in World War II, the *Renown* was broken up for scrap at Faslane in the United Kingdom during 1948.

84

USS *Saratoga*

On 7 February 1928, the Panama Canal was introduced to the size of the modern-day aircraft carrier as the 33,000-ton-displacement USS *Saratoga* transited from the Atlantic to the Pacific. With a length of 888 feet and a beam of 107.9 feet, the *Saratoga* quickly established herself as the longest and widest vessel to have transited the Panama Canal to that date. Originally laid down as a battlecruiser, the *Saratoga* was finished as the first fast (33 knots) carrier of the U.S. Navy. She was followed into service by the USS *Lexington*, which transited the Panama Canal in March of 1928, a passage that resulted in a number of damaged lamp posts along one lock, caused by the carrier's expansive flight deck. In the prewar years, the *Saratoga* and *Lexington* were used in a number of naval exercises to determine the value of aircraft carriers in modern warfare. The results established the versatility and power of a fast naval task force centered around an aircraft carrier, but the implications were sometimes forgotten. Only three years before the Japanese launched their attack on Pearl Harbor, the *Saratoga* carried out a similar and successful test exercise from a launching point 100 miles off Oahu. The *Saratoga* lived on to survive the war, earning seven battle stars, but was sunk as a test ship at Bikini Atoll in July of 1946. During her career she established a record for the greatest number of aircraft landed on a carrier, 98,549 landings, in the space of 17 years.

Asama

Bearing a strong resemblance to a floating laundry, the Japanese armored cruiser *Asama* transits through Gaillard Cut on 22 October 1929. The elderly warship, already well past her prime, was acting as a cadet training vessel and had a number of young men on board who would no doubt later be drawn into the holocaust of World War II. On this trip the *Asama* had visited New York in company with the cruiser *Iwate* and was on her way back to Japan via Mazatlán, Mexico. Built just before the turn of the century, the *Asama* was one of Japan's "Elswick" series, having been constructed at the yard of Armstrong, Whitworth & Co., Elswick, in the United Kingdom. As launched, the warship had a displacement of 10,519 tons, a length of 442 feet, a beam of 67 feet and a draft of 24 feet 4 inches. Her original armament was composed of four 8-inch/40-cal guns, fourteen 6-inch/40-cal quickfire (QF) guns, twelve 3-inch QF, eight 47-mm guns, three machine guns, and five 18-inch torpedo tubes. This was updated in 1922 to include eight 3-inch/40-cal guns and one 3.1-inch/40-cal AA. The *Asama* would survive the Second World War as she had World War I and the Russo-Japanese War. In the latter conflict, the cruiser had formed part of the main battle line at Tsushima. In World War II, the British-built vessel was confined to training midshipmen at Kure, then at Osaka and finally at Shimonoseki, where she was surrendered in August of 1945. Two years later the 48-year-old veteran was taken to Hitachi and broken up for scrap.

HMS *Despatch*

The British light cruiser HMS *Despatch* is caught by the camera on 25 January 1930 at Paraiso. The warship had left Bermuda on January 11th for a voyage to South American west coast ports via Kingston, Jamaica. After a four-day stay at Balboa, the ship cleared for Iquique, Chile, on January 29th, touching at Valparaiso, Coquimbo, and Callao before returning to Panama on March 28th. One of a large number of small British cruisers laid down during World War I, the *Despatch* was not completed until 1922. The 4,850-ton vessel carried six 6-inch guns in single turrets, three 4-inch guns, four 3-pounders, twelve guns of smaller caliber, and twelve torpedo tubes in sets of three. Two of the torpedo-tube sets can be seen under canvas awnings amidships. One deck above these units are the two amidships-mounted 6-inch turrets, one forward of the funnels and one abaft. Equipped with steam turbine engines, the light cruiser was capable of 29 knots. Following completion, the *Despatch* served with the 5th Cruiser Squadron in China until 1927 when she became flagship of the 8th Cruiser Squadron, North American and West Indies Station. The ship returned to Chatham, England, in 1931 for a refit. Following this she was attached to the 3rd Cruiser Squadron in the Mediterranean. During World War II the warship operated in a variety of areas, returning to the Caribbean with the 8th Cruiser Squadron during 1941/42. After serving as an accommodation vessel at Portsmouth, England, at war's end, the *Despatch* was sold for scrap on 5 April 1946.

HMS *Nelson*

Resembling a floating fortress shrouded in secrecy, the British battleship *Nelson* transits through Gaillard Cut on 23 February 1931. Under the command of Admiral Sir Michael Hodges, the *Nelson* was proceeding as far as Balboa, where she would be paying a formal call to the U.S. Fleet, which was then resting at anchor after maneuvers in Panama Bay. The *Nelson* had been launched in 1925 and completed in 1927 as one of Britain's largest warships. Her unique design, shared with sister ship *Rodney*, incorporated nine 16-inch guns mounted in three turrets concentrated on the foredeck. This grouping allowed sufficient armor protection to be built up around the turret bases, something which, under the displacement restrictions then in force, would not have been possible with a more normal distribution. Canvas awnings, rigged to provide shade, hide the two lower 16-inch turrets in this picture. Ships of the *Nelson* class were originally designed as 48,000-ton battlecruisers, but construction plans were revised after the Washington Treaty of 1922 placed a 35,000-ton standard displacement limit on all new capital ships. The *Nelson*, consequently, emerged approximately 200 feet shorter than originally planned and with a standard displacement of only 33,313 tons. On this transit the warship displaced 36,640 tons loaded and paid tolls amounting to $18,320. Returning through the canal on February 28th, the battleship displaced 36,494 tons and paid tolls of $18,247. The smaller displacement tonnage was occasioned by less fuel aboard. Both the *Nelson* and *Rodney* survived World War II and were broken up for scrap in 1948/49.

USS *Constitution*

Between 1 July 1931 and 7 May 1934, the U.S. Navy's 1797-built frigate *Constitution* visited 90 U.S. ports along the Atlantic, Pacific, and Gulf coasts; thousands of Americans were able to see the historic vessel. Famed in history as "Old Ironsides," the veteran warship arrived at Cristóbal from Guantánamo Bay, Cuba, on 22 December 1932 under tow of the U.S. Navy minesweeper *Grebe*. This photograph, taken at Pedro Miguel on 27 December 1932, shows the then 135-year-old sailing ship being assisted through the lock by the Panama Canal tug *Tavernilla* and followed by the *Grebe*. Having spent Christmas Day at Cristóbal, the *Constitution* was still decorated with Christmas trees, which can be seen on all three masts and at the tip of her bowsprit. The *Constitution*'s transit of the canal, although exercised with considerable caution, was made in the relatively short time of 9 hours and 23 minutes. Crowds gathered at all viewing places to see the famous ship handled through. After being made available for public inspection at Balboa, the frigate was placed in the Balboa dry dock for examination prior to her onward trip to San Diego. Completely restored during the years preceding her national tour, the *Constitution* was found to be in excellent condition, requiring only a few minor voyage repairs. Following her exhibit along the Pacific coast, the well-known vessel returned through Panama and reached Boston Harbor on 7 May 1934. The *Constitution* remains in commission today, the oldest ship on the United States Navy List.

USS *Houston*

On 11 July 1934 President Franklin Delano Roosevelt was aboard the U.S. cruiser *Houston* as it transited the Panama Canal en route from Annapolis, Maryland, to Portland, Oregon. This was the first passage through the canal by a president of the United States while in office. Military honors were rendered at Miraflores as the warship paused before locking down to the Pacific. The *Houston* had embarked Roosevelt and his party at Annapolis on July 1st, proceeding to the canal via Cape Haitien, Mayaguez, San Juan, St. Thomas, St. Croix, and Cartagena. After a day tour at Balboa on the 12th, the president re-embarked the *Houston*, and the cruiser got under way at 5:30 P.M. for Portland via Cocos Island and Honolulu. While in office, President Roosevelt was to make four more visits to Panama, two aboard the *Houston* in 1935 and 1938 and two aboard the cruiser *Tuscaloosa* in 1940. The *Houston*, launched by Newport News Shipbuilding & Dry Dock Co. in 1929, made her final transit of the canal in 1939. A year later the ship was posted to the Philippines as flagship of the Asiatic Fleet. Following several combat actions against the Japanese during the first few weeks of World War II, the *Houston* was lost in the Battle of the Java Sea in late February 1942. Having battled against far superior forces, the heavy cruiser became one of the most honored ships of the war, winning two battle stars and a Presidential Unit Citation.

HMS *Exeter*

Completed in July 1931, the British cruiser HMS *Exeter* was a relatively new ship when photographed at Gamboa Signal Station on 8 March 1935. At the time, the vessel was returning to Bermuda from a goodwill trip along the west coast of South America. Behind the warship's funnels two float aircraft can be seen mounted on catapults. The *Exeter* was a scaled-down version of the British County-class cruiser, thirteen of which were built following World War I. Unlike her larger sisters, which averaged over 9,750 tons displacement and carried eight 8-inch guns as main armament, the *Exeter* displaced 8,390 tons and carried six 8-inch guns. Her machinery, consisting of 4-shaft Parsons geared turbines, developed 80,000 shaft horsepower and provided a maximum speed of 32.25 knots. In 1939, only a few years after this picture was taken, the British ship took part in the famous action against the German pocket-battleship *Admiral Graf Spee* in the South Atlantic. Though very badly damaged by her adversary's 11-inch guns, the *Exeter*, along with the light cruisers *Ajax* and *Achilles*, emerged victorious in this engagement. Two years later the odds against the *Exeter* were to be overwhelming. While trying to make an Australian port after the disastrous Battle of the Java Sea, the badly damaged *Exeter* came up against a squadron of Japanese warships and was repeatedly shelled. With no ammunition remaining, the dying cruiser was scuttled by her own crew, going down quickly after a final Japanese torpedo hit. Fifty-four officers and men were lost.

3

Passenger Ships and Yachts

Regular passenger-ship services to Panama were inaugurated well before the French began their first canal project on the isthmus in 1880. In the 1840s the Pacific Steam Navigation Company and the Royal Mail Steam Packet Company, both of Great Britain, established services connecting Panama with England, the Caribbean islands, and the west coast of South America. In that same decade, the Pacific Mail Steamship Company was organized to carry passengers and mail from Panama along the west coast of the United States to Oregon.

In later years the newly constructed Panama Railroad created its own steamship line. Many of the company's ships would play an important role in the American effort at Panama. European companies would also begin services to the isthmus, including Germany's Hamburg-American Line and the French Cie. Generale Transatlantique. By 1913 over a dozen shipping firms were sending a total of 35 to 37 regularly scheduled passenger steamers to the Atlantic and Pacific terminals of the Panama Railroad every month. When the waterway opened in 1914, several of these lines expanded their services, and other companies later joined in the competition. The passenger vessels that transited through Panama were not of the size seen on the North Atlantic. For the most part they were small ships, many handling mail and freight as well as passengers. Representative were the 3,406-ton *City of Para* of the Pacific Mail Steamship Company, the 4,858-ton *Santa Teresa* of W.R. Grace & Company, and the 7,827-ton *Orcana* of the Pacific Steam Navigation Company.

When big liners made their appearance at the isthmus, it was usually in the course of a round-the-world or round–South America cruise. Such was the case of the first liner over 10,000 tons to cross Panama, International Mercantile Marine Company's 12,760-ton *Kroonland*. When launched at Philadelphia in 1902, the vessel was the largest American steamship afloat. The *Kroonland* transited from Kingston, Jamaica, to Callao, Peru, on 2 February 1915 with 270 passengers aboard on a round–South America cruise. The regularly scheduled passenger liners making use of the canal continued to increase in size, but they were never able to match the leviathans of the North Atlantic, several of which began transiting Panama on globe-circling luxury cruises each winter during the early 1920s. The first such giant, Cunard's new 19,680-ton *Laconia*, passed through the canal southbound on 29 November 1922. On 16 January 1923, came United American Lines' 19,653-ton *Resolute*, flying the flag of Panama to avoid U.S. prohibition laws. Canadian Pacific's 18,357-ton *Empress of France* followed on 30 January 1923, and Cunard's 19,602-ton *Samaria* transited on 25 May 1923. The big ships, though infrequent visitors, paid high tolls ($47,695 for the above four vessels alone) and brought the glamorous and wealthy to Panama, if only for brief periods of time.

It was on the smaller, more frequently seen liners, however, that the population of the isthmus and the work force of the Panama Canal depended for transportation. The Panama Railroad built up its own fleet of steamers through the construction era of the canal. It offered canal employees and their dependents a flat-rate fare of $20 between Cristóbal and New York, where the company used Pier 67 on the North River. Other passengers were charged $100 (first class) for the eight-day voyage, which included a stop at Haiti. Accommodation aboard a Panama Railroad ship, even in first class, was not overly luxurious. A typical cabin on the 3,150-ton *Allianca*, one of the line's older steamers, measured only six and a half feet by seven feet. It was furnished with a double set of bunks measuring two feet three inches wide along one wall and an 18-inch wide upholstered bench along the opposite wall. Space between the bunks and the bench was little more than three feet. There were no wardrobes, tables, or chairs. Each cabin contained a wash basin, but the lavatories, showers, and bathtubs were located down the passageway.

Somewhat better cabins could be obtained for around $145 on the steamers of competing companies, including the Pacific Mail Steamship Company and Grace Line. The white-hulled banana boats of the United Fruit Company could also be taken to New York, although the voyage might be interrupted by stops at several Central American or Caribbean ports along the way. In 1923, the Boston-based fruit company charged $25 for an overnight trip north to Limón, Costa Rica. A two-day voyage to Tela in Honduras was $60. Havana could be reached for $75 and New Orleans, a five-day trip, was $110. A United Fruit steamer such as the Dutch-built *Saramacca*, though designed to carry over 40,000 stems of bananas in refrigerated holds, could also accommodate 40 passengers in relative comfort.

Other companies, including Elders & Fyffes of the United Kingdom, accommodated passengers on their ships operating to and from the isthmus. A berth in a well-appointed cabin on the 100-passenger-capacity *Ariguani* from Cristóbal to Bristol could be fetched for $240. Liverpool and London were reachable on ships of Pacific Steam Navigation for $230, while Southampton was served by the New Zealand Shipping Company and Shaw, Savill & Albion for $250. If one wasn't financially up to a first-class passage, a third-class berth between the isthmus and Southampton on the British ships was only $100.

Passenger traffic continued to build across the isthmus through the 1920s. In the period of 1 December 1922 until 30 April 1923, 39,170 passengers arrived at Panama and 38,938 departed. By the same period during 1925–26, the figures had climbed to 52,601 arriving and 52,257 departing. Five around-the-world cruise ships passed through the canal during the latter period carrying a total of 1,847 through passengers. The *Belgenland, Laconia, Resolute, Empress of Scotland,* and *Franconia* all transited from the Atlantic to the Pacific and paid almost $70,000 in aggregate tolls. The cruise ship visits were to taper off with the coming of the depression, as were calls by scheduled liners. During the month of December 1929, nine large tourist vessels called at Panama—the *Carinthia, Franconia, Reliance, Resolute, Statendam, Kungsholm, Belgenland,* and *Duchess of Bedford.* A total of 3,150 passengers had been booked on these vessels, but by the time the ships sailed, only 2,354 passengers were on board. The sudden cancellation of over 25 percent of the reservations was attributed to the falling off of business in the United States.

Ernest Hallen took his last photograph of a large liner at Panama on 5 May 1935, when the 42,348-ton *Empress of Britain* transited north on one of its final world cruises. He was to miss the record-setting visit of the 51,731-ton *Bremen* on 15 February 1939, a passenger ship that was not to be exceeded in size at Panama for well over three and a half decades.

Allianca

In 1914, as the date for the Panama Canal's official opening grew close, a number of test transits were undertaken to make sure all equipment was in order. On the morning of 8 June 1914, the Panama Railroad steamer *Allianca* passed through Gatun Locks from the Atlantic to Gatun Lake. In doing so, the little ship became the first oceangoing passenger vessel to enter or pass through any of the canal lock systems. The *Allianca* arrived off Gatun at 6:45 A.M. and was taken in hand by four canal towing locomotives, Nos. 641, 642, 643, and 644. This photograph, showing the vessel about to leave the upper lock chamber and enter Gatun Lake, was taken at approximately 8:40 that morning. The tug *Cocoli* accompanied the *Allianca* throughout her transit. Workers and their families, dressed in their Sunday best, were on hand to see the passenger ship handled through. The *Allianca* stayed in Gatun Lake for one hour before returning through the locks to the Atlantic. (On June 11th the steamer *Ancon* made a similar test run in preparation for her own history-making Atlantic to Pacific crossing on August 15th.) Built in 1886, The *Allianca* had been obtained from the United States & Brazil Mail Steamship Company in 1895 for operation by the Panama Railroad. The passenger-cargo vessel served the Panama Railroad for many years, opening up a new route for the company from New York to Guayaquil in 1920. After 37 years of service, the ship was sold to the Boston Iron and Metals Company for scrap in 1923.

104

Cristobal

Before the steamship *Ancon* officially opened the Panama Canal on 15 August 1914, her sister ship, the *Cristobal*, made a test transit over the waterway's entire length. This photograph, taken on the morning of 3 August 1914, captures the Panama Railroad vessel as she was leaving Gatun Locks southbound. Behind the steamer is one of six rotatable emergency dams installed at the six uppermost lock chambers along the canal to guard against possible lock gate failure. When the *Cristobal* left Miraflores Locks and entered the Pacific later that day, she became the first large oceangoing vessel to transit the canal's entire length. The unofficial but history-making trip was followed by similar test transits involving the ships *Advance* and *Panama* on August 9th and 11th. Guest passengers were carried on these short voyages, but no cargo. On August 15th, with much fanfare, the *Ancon* was locked through with 200 passengers, plus cargo destined for transshipment at Balboa. This was considered the first official transit of the Panama Canal by a steamship engaged in commercial service. On this first transit of the canal by the *Cristobal*, the ship was handled through by lock's personnel, but after a locomotive motor was ruined and a cable snapped, it was decided that a professional pilot force would be needed to guide ships through. Captain John A. Constantine became the first member of this elite group when he took the steamer *Ancon* through the canal without incident on August 15th.

106

Ceramic

On a rainy day in December 1917, the White Star liner *Ceramic* made a northbound transit of the canal en route from Australia to the United Kingdom. Around the forward towing locomotive several workers can be seen holding umbrellas. Most, however, make do with the lee side of a lamppost for protection. A lady in white shelters at the staircase in front of the ship. Note the sheds that have been built on the *Ceramic*'s boat deck just below the wheelhouse, possibly for the transport of horses. Launched in 1912 and built for a cost of 436,000 pounds sterling, the 18,481-ton *Ceramic* was for many years the largest vessel operating to Australia. Her cargo capacity was 836,000 cubic feet in eight holds. Of this, 321,000 cu. ft. were refrigerated. The vessel also had accommodation for 600 third-class passengers, but through the war years she normally sailed only as a cargo carrier. When White Star moved out of the Australian trade in the early 1930s, the *Ceramic* was sold to Shaw, Savill & Albion, who had the vessel reconstructed at Govan in 1936. The 679-foot liner emerged with a slightly faster service speed and a passenger capacity reduced to 480, all in cabin class. On 7 December 1942, while bound from Liverpool to Australia, the *Ceramic* was torpedoed and sunk by German submarine U-515 just west of the Azores. Of 656 people aboard the ship, only one man survived. The U-515 was hunted down by American destroyers and her master, Captain Lieutenant W. Henke, captured. He was later killed while attempting to escape from a prisoner-of-war camp.

Callao

The *Callao*, shown in this photograph at Balboa's Pier 8 during early April of 1918, was originally the North German Lloyd liner *Sierra Cordoba* built in 1912. At the start of World War I, the 8,226-ton ship had been interned by the government of Peru while anchored in Peruvian waters. Following negotiations between U.S. and Peruvian authorities, the vessel was towed north to the Panama Canal workshops for conversion to a U.S. troop ship. The liner had been heavily damaged by her German crew in an attempt to render the ship unfit for further service. Many fittings had been dismantled and thrown overboard. Other vital parts had been smashed or broken. The Balboa shops undertook approximately 400 separate jobs on the vessel to repair the damage. Within six months of her arrival, the German liner was again ready for service. On 7 April 1919, the rebuilt vessel sailed for New York as the *Callao* to take up trooping duties across the Atlantic. When her government employment was over, the steamer was sold to Robert Dollar & Co. and renamed *Ruth Alexander*. America's entrance into World War II found the 30-year-old vessel loading in the Philippines under the command of Captain F. P. Willarts. The *Ruth Alexander* made an escape bid to Australia with several other ships, but was bombed and sunk by Japanese aircraft in the Celebes Sea on 9 January 1942. One man was lost. The remaining 46 crew members were rescued by Dutch Dornier flying boats and safely landed at Balikpapan on the nearby island of Borneo.

110

City of Para

One of the oldest vessels to use the Panama Canal on a regular basis, the 3,406-ton *City of Para* is seen passing Gold Hill on 15 May 1920. The ship was built in 1878 by John Roach and Sons, Chester, Pennsylvania, for the United States and Brazil Mail Steamship Company. Following three years of service with that firm, the liner was purchased by Pacific Mail Steamship Company for $450,000 and placed in service between New York and Colón. Only a few months prior to this transaction, the first group of French engineers had landed at Colón to begin construction of what was to be the "Canal Interoceanique." In 1888, the year the French attempt at Panama went broke, the *City of Para* stranded on Old Providence Island in the Caribbean. Her passengers were taken off by the steamer S.S. *Madrid*, and the ship itself was saved by the salvage vessel *I.J. Merritt*. After repairs at New York, the *City of Para* returned to her trade, transferring to Pacific service in 1895/96. The 26-year-old steamer was still going strong when the American engineers arrived at Panama in 1904. In an effort to win Canal Company business, Pacific Mail offered a 25 percent reduction for canal employees on its $85 cabin-class fare between Balboa and San Francisco. Accommodation was available on the *City of Para* for 70 cabin and 44 steerage passengers. The steamer was finally laid up at San Francisco in 1921 after 43 years of service. Three years later the iron-hulled vessel was sold for scrap, making her final voyage from Hampton Roads to Venice, Italy, in June of 1924 with a full cargo of coal on board.

Essequibo

Photographed on 10 September 1921 in Miraflores Locks, the liner *Essequibo* was en route from New York to Valparaiso. Though launched in 1914 for the West Indies service of the Royal Mail Line, the ship made only a few runs to the Caribbean before being requisitioned by the British government for use as a hospital ship during World War I. Following war service, the *Essequibo* and her sister vessel, the *Ebro*, were transferred to the New York–South America west coast service of the Pacific Steam Navigation Company. The *Ebro* first transited the canal southbound on 28 October 1919, while the *Essequibo* followed on 10 July 1920. Stiff competition was provided on this route by American companies, but the *Essequibo* managed to become the first vessel to transport fresh fruit from Chile to New York in April of 1921. This became an important and profitable trade, but in the late 1920s a worldwide depression put a damper on any further expansion in this area. In November of 1930 the management of the Pacific Steam Navigation Company notified its shippers that the *Ebro* and *Essequibo* were being temporarily taken out of service. The *Ebro* made its last northbound transit of the canal on 14 November 1930. Neither ship ever returned. After several years of lay-up in England, the *Ebro* went on to become the Yugoslavian *Princesa Olga* and then the Portuguese *Serpa Pinto*. She was finally scrapped in 1955. The *Essequibo* entered the merchant marine of the Soviet Union in 1935 as the *Neva* and was later converted into a submarine tender for the Russian Pacific Fleet. The vessel was reported to have been scrapped during the 1970s.

114

Cuba

The 3,241-ton *Cuba*, photographed southbound in the east chamber of Pedro Miguel Lock on 13 October 1921, was a frequent visitor to Panama. The vessel had been built by Blohm & Voss, Hamburg, in 1897 as the *Coblenz*, but during World War I had been taken over by the United States Shipping Board and renamed *Sachem*. On 6 February, 1920 the steamer was sold by the Shipping Board to the Pacific Mail Steamship Company for $400,000 and shortly thereafter renamed *Cuba*. For several months she operated on Pacific Mail's service between San Francisco and Havana carrying cargo and passengers. In February 1921 the ship was transferred to the company's San Francisco/Cristóbal service to run alongside the *Newport*, *San Juan*, and *San Jose*. When the *San Jose* was lost on 9 August 1921, a second German vessel, the 1905-built *Corinto*, ex-*Caldas*, was purchased to fill the gap. Together, the four small cargo-passenger liners offered a service every 15 days between Panama and the North American west coast via Central American and Mexican ports. Most sailings connected at Cristóbal with onward services of Pacific Mail and other steamship lines to the U.S. East Coast and Europe. On 8 September 1923, while on a northbound voyage between Panama and San Francisco with a cargo of coffee, sugar, mahogany, and bullion, the *Cuba* went aground on the southeast tip of San Miguel Island in the Santa Barbara Channel. All 112 people aboard were removed safely, but the *Cuba*, insured for $319,917.17, was a total loss.

Orcana

With a clipper bow from an earlier era, the Pacific Steam Navigation Company liner *Orcana* approaches Pedro Miguel Lock from Valparaiso on the morning of 13 October 1921. On the liner's bridge the captain and pilot oversee proceedings as two towing locomotives prepare to take up slack lines. Passengers watch from covered decks, while several of the ship's crew work forward. A canal crane boat, quite possibly the French-built *Alexandre La Valley*, approaches from the rear. The *Orcana* had been built as the *Miltiades* in 1903 by Alexander Stephen & Sons, Glasgow, for the United Kingdom-Australia service of the Aberdeen Line. In 1912 the ship was lengthened by 50 feet and a second funnel added, a move that altered the ship's profile, increased its passenger capacity, and boosted the vessel's gross registered tonnage. Nine years later the 7,827-ton liner, along with its sister, the *Marathon*, was acquired by the Pacific Steam Navigation Company to replace three of its larger ships, the *Orduna*, *Orbita*, and *Oropesa*, which were transferred to the Royal Mail Line. The *Orcana* and *Marathon* (renamed *Oruba*), along with several other ships of the P.S.N.C., provided a regular service between England and the west coast of South America via Panama. Passenger tickets between Cristóbal and Liverpool were $230 first class, $129 second class, $96 intermediate class, and $72 third class. Though the prices fit all purses, the *Orcana* and *Oruba* proved too expensive to operate. In 1924 the *Oruba* was withdrawn and sent to the breakers, followed one year later by the *Orcana*.

Buckeye State

One of sixteen "535"-type ships ordered by the U.S. government during World War I, the *Buckeye State* was launched by the Bethlehem Shipbuilding Corporation at Sparrows Point, Maryland, in 1920. Ships of this class, measuring 535 feet in overall length, were larger and more powerful versions of the 502 class, which measured 502 feet between perpendiculars. In 1921 shortly after completion, the *Buckeye State* was handed over to the Matson Navigation Company for a new service from the U.S. East Coast to Hawaii via the Panama Canal. The liner departed Baltimore on its first sailing for Matson 21 June 1921. A second "535" type, the *Hawkeye State*, had departed for Hawaii under Matson management a few months earlier. Though well advertised, the austere-looking ships never realized their full potential. Passenger loads were light and mechanical troubles frequent. In 1922 both ships were handed back to the U.S. Shipping Board after only a few voyages. The *Buckeye State* is pictured on her last southbound voyage for Matson, passing through Gaillard Cut 14 January 1922. The liner was subsequently taken over by the Pacific Mail Steamship Company as the *President Taft* and later became part of the Dollar Line and American President Line fleets under that same name. In 1941 the ship was converted into the military transport *Willard A. Holbrook*. Surviving World War II, the 37-year-old liner was broken up for scrap in 1957. The *Hawkeye State* was not so lucky. She was renamed *President Pierce* in 1922, then converted into the Navy transport *Hugh L. Scott* during 1941. The vessel was sunk off North Africa by U-130 on 12 November 1942.

Empress of Australia

On 1 July 1922 the *Empress of Australia* arrived at Cristóbal from Hamburg, Germany, where the 21,860-ton vessel had undergone alterations for transpacific service. Following minor repairs at Cristóbal, the ship transited the canal in ballast on the 6th of July en route to Vancouver, Canada. She is shown at Paraiso after having just passed the northbound tanker *Benjamin Brewster*, en route from Talara to New York. Launched by Germany in 1913 as the *Admiral von Tirpitz*, the liner was not completed until 1920, after which she was handed over to Great Britain for use as a troop transport. On 25 July 1921 the ship was sold to Canadian Pacific and renamed *Empress of China*. Following her 1922 refit, the name was changed to *Empress of Australia*. On 1 September 1923, during a call at Yokohama, Japan, the passenger liner was caught up in the great Tokyo earthquake. Though swept against another vessel, the *Empress of Australia* was eventually brought under control with the assistance of a passing Dutch oil tanker. Five years later, on 5 April 1928, the passenger vessel made her second transit of the Panama Canal while on an around-the-world cruise out of New York. In the previous year the ship had entered the transatlantic trade, sailing between Quebec and Southampton during the summer months. This employment lasted until the start of World War II, when the *Empress of Australia* became a British troop transport, a duty that was prolonged until well after the war. In 1952 the 39-year-old ship was sold for scrap in Great Britain.

Laconia

The first ship on a round-the-world cruise to pass through the Panama Canal was the 1921-built *Laconia*. The 19,680-ton Cunard liner transited from the Atlantic to the Pacific on Wednesday 29 November 1923. She was on a world tour conducted by the American Express Company with 356 tourists aboard. This "first" at Panama aroused some interest among the local population, and both the ship and its passengers were given a royal welcome. Reciprocating, the Cunard Line invited the governor of the Panama Canal and other prominent officials aboard the *Laconia* for the transit through to Pedro Miguel Lock. At the lock, a gangplank was put in place allowing the party and various members of the ship's company to disembark for an auto tour of Panama City. After re-embarking her passengers that evening, the *Laconia* sailed for California, Japan, China, the Philippines, Malaya, Java, Ceylon, Suez, the Mediterranean, Great Britain, and New York. Though the Cunarder was to return to Panama several times, she was not to survive World War II. Acting as a troop transport in 1942, the *Laconia* was torpedoed and sunk off West Africa by German submarine U-156. Over 2,700 people were aboard—among them 1,793 Italian prisoners of war. When it was realized that Italian troops were drowning, a massive rescue effort was attempted by the German submarine and other Axis vessels in the area. This effort was abandoned after several of the ships were bombed by U.S. aircraft. During the rescue operations, however, over 1,000 people were saved, including about 400 Italians.

Santa Teresa

A product of W. Cramp & Sons Shipbuilding, Philadelphia, the 4,858-ton *Santa Teresa* was launched in 1918 for the South American services of W. R. Grace & Co., whose Grace Line was one of the principal users of the Panama Canal. A small ship, the *Santa Teresa* nevertheless had accommodation for 114 passengers and space for considerable freight. Photographed on 13 March 1923, the liner was transiting from New York to Talcahuano, Chile, with 2,470 tons of general cargo on board. In the previous year the *Santa Teresa* had made 12 transits of the canal. Only two other ships had accomplished a greater number of crossings during 1922, the Standard Oil tanker *Benjamin Brewster*, which completed 13 transits between Peru and North America, and the small Colombian steamer *Balboa*, which crossed the isthmus 17 times while engaged in the Colombian intercoastal trade. The *Santa Teresa* remained a steady customer of the Panama locks until superseded by larger and faster Grace ships in the mid-1930s. In 1936 the *Santa Teresa* was sold to the Merchants & Miners Transportation Company of New York, who refitted the liner for employment under the name *Kent*. Five years later the vessel was taken over by the U.S. government for service as the army hospital ship *Ernest Hinds*. When no further commercial employment could be found at the end of World War II, the *Ernest Hinds* was laid up. Though kept afloat in the U.S. government's reserve fleet for many years, the 39-year-old ship was finally scrapped at Baltimore during 1957.

Finland

The 12,760-ton *Finland* was launched at Philadelphia on 2 June 1902 by Cramp for the Red Star Line of New York. For over a decade the liner operated across the North Atlantic between New York and Europe, but in May of 1915 she was engaged by the Panama-Pacific Line to operate between New York and San Francisco. The *Finland* made her first trip through the Panama Canal on 7 May 1915, but was then returned to the North Atlantic because of earth slides that closed the canal to navigation until April 1916. Following service during World War I as a U.S. Navy transport, the *Finland* was rebuilt as a passenger ship and returned to North Atlantic service in 1919. In the fall of 1923 both the *Finland* and sistership *Kroonland* were sold to the Panama-Pacific Line, which again commenced its intercoastal operations between New York and San Francisco. This 5 December 1923 photograph shows the *Finland* transiting the canal on return from her first postwar voyage to San Francisco, with several hundred passengers and 2,150 tons of general cargo aboard. In 1924 the Panama-Pacific Line added San Diego, California, to its schedule; the port was called at 15 days out of New York. The Panama-Pacific Line also served Havana and Los Angeles, operating approximately 19 round-trip voyages each year. During her lifetime, the *Finland* completed 32 of these voyages and paid a grand total of $572,203.75 in Panama Canal tolls. The ship made her final transit of Panama on 14 March 1928 en route to New York and then to Blyth, England, for breaking.

Rotorua

Flying the banner of the New Zealand Shipping Company of London, the 12,184-ton liner *Rotorua* is seen transiting Pedro Miguel Locks on a southbound voyage from England to New Zealand in late 1923. One of a class of three ships launched in 1911 by John Brown, Clydebank, the *Rotorua* was built as the *Shropshire* for the Federal Steam Navigation Company. With accommodations for 130 first-class passengers, the *Shropshire* operated a regular service with her sister vessel, the *Wiltshire*, between Liverpool and Brisbane. In 1914 the ships were taken over by the British government for use as troop transports, duty which they both survived. After being badly damaged by a fire in 1921, the *Shropshire* was fully reconditioned and converted over to oil-firing. Renamed *Rotorua*, the vessel made its first transit of the Panama Canal under N.Z.S.C. colors on 12 April 1923 with 7,922 tons of general cargo, 34 first-class and 383 third-class passengers on board. On a return trip the following July, the *Rotorua* arrived at Balboa carrying 6,600 tons of U.K.-bound cargo. Included in the manifest were 500 tons of beef, 1,600 tons of mutton, 1,000 tons of butter, 1,300 tons of cheese, 400 tons of tallow, and 800 tons of wool, commodities well representative of New Zealand's trade with the world. On 11 December 1940 the *Rotorua* was torpedoed and sunk by the German submarine U-96 off the coast of Scotland. Twenty people lost their lives in the incident. The *Wiltshire* had been lost 18 years earlier in an accident on the New Zealand coast, while a third sister, the *Argyllshire*, was broken up in 1936.

Oroya

Making one of her few profitable voyages, the 12,257-ton British liner *Oroya* is seen on 21 March 1924 transiting between Talcahuano, Chile, and Liverpool with 8,680 tons of cargo aboard. The liner was launched by Harland & Wolff Ltd., Belfast, in 1920 for the Pacific Steam Navigation Company, but was laid up uncompleted for many months because of a shipping slump. It was not until 18 May 1923 that the vessel arrived at Panama on her maiden voyage. Her owning firm, the Pacific Steam Navigation Company, had been founded by an American citizen, William Wheelwright, in the early nineteenth century. Unable to find financial backing in the United States, Mr. Wheelwright eventually registered his new company in the United Kingdom. Vessels of the P.S.N.C. quickly became regular callers at Panama, and for many years the line operated its own repair station on Morro island in Panama Bay. Unfortunately, the 1920s proved to be difficult years for the British firm. In 1922 Chile enacted its own cabotage law, restricting coastal trade to Chilean vessels. In 1929 Peru followed suit, leaving P.S.N.C. with a tonnage surplus. The *Oroya* was laid up in December of 1931 at Dartmouth, along with several of the line's other vessels. Although a few ships were later returned to service, the *Oroya* was not. After seven years of inactivity, the vessel was finally sold. The Dutch tug *Rode Zee* arrived at Dartmouth to take the liner south to Italy for breaking on 1 February 1939, just months before World War II would have required her services.

132

Manchuria

The Panama-Pacific liner *Manchuria* is dressed in white and decorated with signal flags as she transits between San Francisco and New York on 22 October 1924. In the adjacent lock, the American cargo vessel *Margaret Dollar,* built in China during 1921 as the *Celestial*, waits to exit to the Pacific coast. Launched by the New York Shipbuilding Corp., Camden, in November of 1903, the *Manchuria* had an interesting and varied career. Originally designed for North Atlantic service as the *Minnekahda*, the vessel was sold to the Pacific Mail Steamship Company of New York before completion and entered service in 1904 as the *Manchuria*. The 13,639-ton liner sailed between San Francisco and Hong Kong until 1915, when it came under the control of the Atlantic Transport Company, who moved the ship to the North Atlantic. This employment came to an end in 1918 when the *Manchuria* became a U.S. Navy transport. Following the war, the *Manchuria* shifted to the American Line banner and was placed in service between New York and Hamburg. In 1923, the liner was transferred to the Panama-Pacific Line and given a thorough refit at New York. The *Manchuria* joined the Dollar Line fleet in 1928 and in 1929 was renamed *President Johnson*. After military service as a transport during World War II, the ship was sold to Portuguese interests and renamed *Santa Cruz*, for immigrant service between Europe and South America. In 1952 the 49-year-old liner was broken up for scrap at Savona, Italy. The *Margaret Dollar*, renamed *Arkansan* in 1936, was sunk in the Caribbean on 16 June 1942.

Belgenland

On 12 December 1924, Red Star Line's passenger liner *Belgenland* transited the canal with a party of 391 passengers on board, all taking part in an around-the-world cruise managed by the American Express Company. Because of her large size, the *Belgenland* set several new Panama Canal records during her transit. These included ship beam (78.4 feet.), registered gross tonnage (27,132), net tonnage (15,352), and Panama Canal net tonnage (18,847). The ship missed paying a record Panama Canal toll by only $442.50, the sum of $16,855 having been paid some four years previously by the liner *America*. The *Belgenland* led a rather odd career. She was launched by Harland & Wolff, Belfast, in 1914, but as a consequence of naval priorities, was not finished until 1917. When completed, the ship emerged not as a passenger liner, but as a cargo vessel, the *Belgic*, for the White Star Line. Following a period of lay-up in 1921, the ship was again sent back to Harland & Wolff and finally finished and named as originally intended. Operated by the Red Star Line between Europe and the United States for a number of years, the *Belgenland* became a regular winter caller at Panama, transiting through the canal on interocean cruises in 1924, 1925, and 1926. In her final days the ship was sold to the Atlantic Transport Co. of West Virginia and made several more transits of the canal under the name *Columbia* for the Panama-Pacific Line. This service, however, proved unprofitable, and the liner was sold for scrap in the United Kingdom during 1936.

President Van Buren

Taken from the lighthouse at Gatun Locks, this 1920 photograph gives an interesting view of the "502"-class American liner *President Van Buren* transiting southbound. Like other members of her class, the *Van Buren* was laid down for the U.S. Shipping Board in World War I as a transport. When the Armistice was signed in 1918, the vessel was redesigned as a cargo-passenger liner and launched as *Old North State*. The ship was powered by two 4-cylinder, triple-expansion engines driving twin screws that gave a service speed of 14 knots. Cargo capacity was approximately 13,000 tons, including 1,200 tons of refrigerated space. Up to 1,000 tons of coconut oil could be carried in the ship's forward fuel tanks. Cabin passengers were accommodated on three decks of the superstructure, with the upper deck featuring a glass-enclosed promenade. Although placed under the management of the United States Mail Line after her launching in 1920, the *Old North State* made few runs for this financially ailing company. In 1921 the ship was taken over by the United States Lines and in 1922 was renamed *President Van Buren*. A year later the vessel was sold to the Dollar Line, under whose colors it is seen here. In 1938 the Dollar Line was taken over by the U.S. government and renamed American President Lines. The *President Van Buren,* renamed *President Fillmore* in 1940, was drafted by the U.S. Army for transport work soon after America entered World War II. The liner never returned to commercial service and was broken up for scrap at Oakland, California, in 1948.

Empress of France

Dramatically framed by Panama's rugged continental divide, the British liner *Empress of France* steams slowly and majestically between two oceans on 16 May 1925. The ship was on the final leg of a 130-day round-the-world cruise, which had already covered almost 30,000 miles. Once clear of the canal, the ocean liner would proceed on to Havana before arriving back at New York on May 23rd. Two years earlier the *Empress of France* had undertaken a similar cruise for Clark's Tours and drawn over 700 passengers, the largest tour group to have visited Panama to that date. On this 1925 trip she had 284 passengers aboard; the 18,357-ton vessel was not overly crowded. For her short trip across Panama, the *Empress* paid tolls amounting to $11,153.75. Shortly after being launched in 1913 by Beardmore, Glasgow, as the *Alsatian* for Allan Line's transatlantic service, the 20-knot liner had served as flagship of Britain's 10th Cruiser Squadron during World War I while acting as an armed merchant cruiser. When the Allan Line was taken over by Canadian Pacific towards the end of hostilities, the *Alsatian* was renamed *Empress of France*. In her new colors the luxury liner undertook both transatlantic voyages and seasonal cruise work. The small number of passengers on her 1925 world cruise, however, foretold the future. After several shifts of employment, including work in the Pacific, the *Empress of France* was laid up in the United Kingdom during 1931. Three years later she was sold to W.H. Arnott Young & Co. for breaking at Dalmuir.

Mongolia

On 17 March 1926 the liner *Mongolia* transited Panama en route from San Pedro, California, to New York. The ship was carrying several hundred passengers and 6,433 tons of general cargo. This photograph shows the vessel passing Camp Gaillard, which had been the canal administration center of Culebra until 1914. Launched by the New York Shipbuilding Corp., Camden, in July of 1903, the *Mongolia* was a sister to the *Manchuria* and shared a similar history. Like the *Manchuria*, the *Mongolia* was originally designed for service with the Atlantic Transportation Company of West Virginia, but was taken over by the Pacific Mail Line before launching. In 1904 the liner commenced transpacific sailings between San Francisco and Hong Kong, then shifted to the Atlantic in 1915 after being repurchased by the Atlantic Transportation Company. Following war service as a navy transport, the *Manchuria* resumed her commercial operations across the Atlantic under American Line colors until 1923 when taken over by the Panama-Pacific Line for intercoastal work. In 1924 the liner was given a thorough refit, providing accommodation for 267 first-class and 1,370 third-class passengers. Service between New York and San Francisco commenced in 1925. The *Mongolia* made her last transit of the canal in Panama-Pacific Line colors on 9 October 1929, after which she was sold to the Dollar Steamship Line and renamed *President Fillmore*. In 1940 the 37-year-old vessel was sold to Cia. Transatlantica Centroamericana and renamed *Panamanian*. It was under this name that the *Mongolia* was scrapped in the Far East during 1946/47.

142

Ariguani

This photograph of the Elders & Fyffes banana ship *Ariguani* was taken on 1 September 1926 while the vessel was coaling at Cristóbal. Another of the company's ships can be seen lying astern. By this time the coaling facilities at Cristóbal had become quite sophisticated, and as shown, vessels requiring coal could be bunkered "overall" in near-record time. The *Ariguani* is receiving coal through both side ports and a top-side hatch, the starboard side of the vessel being served by a floating barge equipped with four elevators. In this manner, 1,000 tons of coal could be put aboard in one hour. Coal at Cristóbal sold for about $12 per ton in 1926, but was slightly higher if taken from barges and slightly lower if purchased in amounts over 1,200 tons. The *Ariguani* loaded approximately 1,500 tons, for which she paid $16,750. One of a dozen liners built for Elders & Fyffes after the company took over the Caribbean passenger trade of Elder Dempster, the *Ariguani* was launched by A. Stephen & Sons Ltd., Glasgow, in 1926. All twelve ships were twin screwed and could steam at 14 knots. Each vessel had cabin accommodations for 100 passengers and a refrigerated area for 80,000 stems of bananas. The *Ariguani* was nicknamed the "Harry-Go-Hungry" by low-paid British stevedores who unloaded her voluminous cargo of bananas at Avonmouth. In the Caribbean her loaders were even poorer, earning only five pence per 50 stems carried through the side ports. The *Ariguani* survived in her trade until 1956, when she was broken up by T.W. Ward Ltd., Briton Ferry, U.K.

144

City of Los Angeles

A ship with a highly diversified career, the white-hulled liner *City of Los Angeles* is seen on 28 November 1928 passing dredges working at Cucaracha Slide. The passenger vessel was transiting to the Pacific on a 64-day "Round-South-America" cruise that had departed Los Angeles on October 9th. Launched in 1899, the 12,642-ton steamship had been built by Schichau, Danzig, as the German-flag *Grosser Kurfürst*. The vessel operated in transatlantic and Europe-Australia service until 1914. During this period, the ship participated in the rescue of survivors from the British cargo-passenger liner *Volturno* that sank in October 1913. Interned at New York during World War I and later seized by the U.S. government, the *Grosser Kurfürst* was renamed *Aeolus* in 1917 and used as a U.S. Navy transport. After war work, the ship was returned to the U.S. Shipping Board, which chartered the vessel out to Munson Line in 1920. On 20 April 1922 while in South American service, the *Aeolus* rammed and sank the British freighter *Zero* off Uruguay. Two months after this incident, the liner was rechartered to the Los Angeles S.S. Co. for operation between California and the Hawaiian Islands. Renamed *City of Los Angeles*, the ship was fashioned into one of the most luxurious passenger vessels in the Pacific, at a cost of $1,061,065. Displaced by newer tonnage a decade later, the *City of Los Angeles* was laid up in 1932. She was used for two cruises to the South Pacific in 1934, but was sold for breaking in Japan during 1937.

146

President Hayes

The *President Hayes*, an American-flag cargo-passenger liner, was another of the "502-class" ships laid down by the United States toward the end of World War I. Built by the New York Shipbuilding Corp., the 10,533-ton vessel was launched as the *Creole State* on 27 April 1920 and placed under the control of the Pacific Mail Steamship Company. In this employment, the liner first passed through the canal on 3 January 1921 bound from Baltimore for San Francisco via Los Angeles. In the following year the ship was renamed *President Hayes* and switched to the South American trade of Swayne & Hoyt, passing through Panama on 6 February 1923 bound for Brazilian ports. Returning through the canal in April of that year, the *President Hayes* had on board 2,232 tons of coffee, 1,407 tons of fertilizer, 2,000 tons of linseed, and 910 tons of raw hides. This typical South American cargo was augmented at Balboa by 2,265 bunches of Panamanian-grown bananas. Though highly varied, the cargo was not a paying one for a ship of 13,000 tons capacity. Within a year the *President Hayes* was switched to yet another trade route, this time carrying the banner of the Dollar Steamship company around the globe. Inaugurated in February of 1924, the round-the-world service occupied the *President Hayes* until the coming of World War II. In her first 11 circumnavigations of the globe, the American liner covered an aggregate of 281,985 miles and touched at 21 regular ports of call per trip. The *President Hayes* maintained a sailing efficiency of 97 percent per published schedule, which was an unequaled accomplishment at the time. The ship was broken up for scrap at Philadelphia in 1957.

148

Saramacca

Among the regular users of the Panama Canal after 1927, no vessels were as widely known and easily identifiable as those of Boston's United Fruit Company. Known as the "Great White Fleet," the white-hulled "banana boats" of United Fruit became nautical landmarks in the Caribbean. In 1908, shortly after a virulent plant disease wiped out banana plantations in Dutch Guiana, the Boston firm bought four fully refrigerated cargo-passenger ships from the Dutch West Indies Company. Two of these vessels, the *Marowijne* and *Coppename*, had been built by Workman, Clark & Company, Belfast. The other two, *Suriname* and *Saramacca*, had been launched by Nederlandsche Scheepsbouw Maatschappij, Amsterdam. All four ships were put under the American flag and then introduced into service between New Orleans and Central America. In August of 1915 the *Marowijne* disappeared with all on board after tempting fate by sailing from Belize, British Honduras, on Friday, August the 13th. The three remaining ex-Dutch ships led long lives and became familiar callers at Panama. In 1929 the *Saramacca* and *Suriname* were placed on United Fruit's new intercoastal service between San Francisco and New Orleans, replacing the smaller *Limon*, which had inaugurated the run in 1927. This undated photograph, showing the 3,212-ton *Saramacca* transiting southbound at Cucaracha Slide, was probably taken shortly after this change. In 1938, after 30 years of service, the *Saramacca* was sold out of the fleet to Italian interests. Renamed *Argentea*, the ship was destroyed by Allied aircraft on 12 May 1944 and later salvaged for scrap.

Columbus

The North German Lloyd passenger ship *Columbus*, photographed from the vantage point of a floating crane at Paraiso, set several Panama Canal records during her first transit of the waterway on 3 May 1930. On that date, the liner became the largest commercial ship to have transited in point of length (749.6 feet), registered gross tonnage (32,565), registered net tonnage (16,829), and Panama Canal net tonnage (20,079). Oddly enough, although she exceeded the length and gross tonnage of other large ships that had transited Panama, including the *Empress of Scotland, America,* and *Belgenland*, the *Columbus* paid a smaller toll ($15,991.25) because of her United States registry measurement (12,793), on which the canal tolls were figured. A year later the liner again transited Panama on a world cruise with 350 passengers aboard. Laid down just before the start of World War I, the *Columbus* was not fully completed until 1923. Her name was to have been *Hindenburg*, but when a sister vessel, the 1913-built *Columbus*, was transferred to the British flag in 1919, the 1923-built ship was renamed *Columbus*. At the outbreak of World War II, the liner was on a cruise in the Caribbean. After leaving her passengers in Havana, she was sighted and ordered to stop by the British warship HMS *Hyperion*. Before a boarding party could be sent across, the *Columbus* was set afire and scuttled by her own crew, going down some 420 miles southeast of New York City on 19 December 1939. Two men from the ship were reported missing. The rest were taken on board the American cruiser *Tuscaloosa* and landed in the United States.

Rangitata

One of three sister ships built for the New Zealand-United Kingdom trade by John Brown, Clydebank, the 16,737-ton passenger liner *Rangitata* was completed in October of 1929 and made her first transit of the canal on December 9th that same year. She had been preceded through the waterway by the 16,755-ton *Rangitiki*, which reached Panama on 6 March 1929, and was followed by the 16,733-ton *Rangitane* in early January 1930. The *Rangitata* was originally owned by the Federal Steam Navigation Company, while her sisters came under the ownership of the New Zealand Shipping Company. In 1936 *Rangitata* was purchased by the N.Z.S.C., which had operated her for many years. All three ships represented a major investment in the New Zealand trade and joined a series of smaller ships sailing to and from that island country. Passengers joining the liners at Balboa could sail on to Auckland or Wellington, a trip of approximately two weeks duration, for $285 first class, $200 second class, or $125 third class. An unusual stop on this route was tiny Pitcairn Island, which was called at on alternate voyages. World War II was to interrupt this schedule. On 27 November 1940 the *Rangitane*, while bound for Panama from New Zealand, was intercepted by German commerce raiders *Komet* and *Orion*. Shelled and torpedoed in the early morning hours, the large liner quickly sank with the loss of 16 lives. The *Rangitiki* and *Rangitata* survived the war to return to peacetime service in 1948 and 1949. The *Rangitiki* was sold to Spain for breaking in 1962 while the *Rangitata* was broken up that same year in Yugoslavia.

Europa

In the early 1930s the East Asiatic Company of Denmark placed three small two-funneled cargo-passenger liners in service between Europe and the west coast of North America. The second of these ships was the 10,224-ton *Europa*, which arrived at Cristóbal on its maiden voyage during the morning of 8 June 1931. At the time of her arrival, the *Europa* had on board only two tons of cargo for discharge at Cristóbal and 14 through passengers. If the ship had proceeded through the canal with its 14 passengers, the *Europa* would have been considered a "laden" vessel, and the tolls would have amounted to $7,223.75. To save money, the *Europa*'s captain had his 14 passengers disembark with their baggage at Cristóbal and take the train across the isthmus at the ship's expense. Having neither cargo nor passengers aboard, the *Europa* then paid only $5,958 in tolls as it transited "in ballast." The total savings amounted to $1,265.75. At Balboa the passengers reboarded the vessel upon completion of its transit. Shortly after their introduction to service, the three thrifty Danish liners, which could accommodate 52 to 64 passengers in first-class cabins, introduced a series of budget cruises from west coast ports to Panama and the Caribbean. Passengers on these special cruises disembarked at either Cristóbal or St. Thomas in the Virgin Islands outbound, then caught a west-bound ship for their return journey. Though this type of cruise became popular, neither the service nor the ships were to survive World War II. The *Europa*, put under the British flag upon the German occupation of Denmark in 1939, was destroyed in a German air attack on Liverpool in May 1941.

Empress of Britain

The 42,348-ton *Empress of Britain* strikes a calm, prewar pose in Pedro Miguel Locks while on a round-the-world cruise in 1932 with 469 passengers aboard. As the great liner is guided slowly ahead by shepherding mechanical mules, passengers don pith helmets and bonnets to guard against the tropical sun. On the navigation bridge one individual can be seen taking in the scenery while balanced precariously on the port wing house. The *Empress of Britain*, launched in 1930 by John Brown, Clydebank, for Canadian Pacific, reset the Panama Canal record book during her April 1st transit. Her 97-foot 8-inch beam bettered that of Matson Navigation's *Malolo* (83.2 feet), and her registered gross tonnage (42,348), registered net tonnage (22,545), and Panama Canal net (27,503) topped that of previous champion *Columbus* of North German Lloyd. Also broken were two records set by Canadian Pacific's smaller *Empress of Scotland*. The *Empress of Britain* boosted the United States net tonnage record to 15,153 and thus set a new commercial toll high of $18,941.25. The impressive vessel's life was to span but a decade. Converted over to a troop transport at the beginning of World War II, she was spotted by German aircraft off the coast of Ireland on 26 October 1940 and repeatedly bombed. Taken in tow by a Polish destroyer, the unfortunate liner was sunk two days later by German submarine U-32. Her loss set yet another record. The *Empress of Britain* had the dubious honor of becoming the largest merchant vessel to be sunk in the course of World War II.

158

Mataroa

In 1926 the Shaw, Savill & Albion Company chartered two passenger vessels, the *Diogenes* and *Sophocles*, from the Aberdeen Line for service between Great Britain and New Zealand. The twin ships had been built by Harland & Wolff, Belfast, in 1922 as replacements for the old Aberdeen Line steamers *Miltiades* and *Marathon,* which were subsequently traded to the Pacific Steam Navigation Company. For their new service, the *Diogenes* and *Sophocles* were renamed *Mataroa* and *Tamaroa* and were converted from coal to oil burning, an alteration that gave each ship an increase in speed of 1.5 knots. The 12,354-ton *Tamaroa* first sailed under Shaw, Savill & Albion colors from Southampton on 10 September 1926. The 12,333-ton *Mataroa* followed several weeks later, passing through Panama on 21 November 1926 with 672 passengers and 5,800 tons of cargo on board. In 1931, passenger accommodation aboard both liners was reduced to 130 in cabin class only, the former third class being eliminated. When the Aberdeen Line came under Shaw, Savill & Albion control one year later, the two vessels were purchased outright. This photograph, taken on 11 March 1933, shows the *Mataroa* passing through Gaillard Cut while on a voyage from London to Port Chalmers with passengers and 1,870 tons of general cargo and automobiles on board. The *Mataroa* and *Tamaroa* both survived World War II, during which they operated as military transports. In 1948 the ships were returned to the New Zealand trade and served without incident until broken up in 1957, the *Mataroa* at Faslane and the *Tamaroa* at Blyth.

Santa Elena

The American passenger liner *Santa Elena* steamed through Gaillard Cut on 8 April 1933 looking very much like the new ship she was. The 9,135-ton vessel had been completed only a few months earlier by Federal Shipbuilding & Drydock Co., Kearny, N.J., and was on her maiden voyage—a three-week passage between New York and Seattle, Washington. The last of four modern turbo-electric liners built for the Grace Line-Panama Mail intercoastal service in the early 1930s, the *Santa Elena* was following sisters *Santa Rosa, Santa Paula,* and *Santa Lucia* out to the west coast. Each ship had accommodation for 222 first-class, 28 third-class, and 36 steerage passengers, as well as space for considerable freight. On this first trip, the *Santa Elena* was carrying 3,680 tons of general cargo and coffee, some of which had been transshipped at New York. With the coming of World War II, the four Grace liners were pressed into service as military transports. Two were lost in combat. On 9 November 1942, the *Santa Lucia*, as the troopship *Leedstown*, was sunk by German aircraft off Algeria. One year later, on November 6th, the *Santa Elena* was caught in the same area and destroyed by German aircraft. Though over 1,800 Canadian troops were on board the *Santa Elena* at the time, the majority were rescued by the Matson liner *Monterey*. Sailing in submarine-infested waters, the *Monterey* and her courageous crew managed to pick up 1,675 survivors in one of the largest rescue operations carried out by a single vessel during the course of World War II.

162

Ionic

One of three nearly identical ships completed in 1902 by Harland & Wolff for Britain's White Star Line, the 12,232-ton *Ionic* is seen passing the old Gamboa Signal Station in November of 1933. The 14-knot vessel was making a northbound transit on a voyage from Wellington, New Zealand, to London with 5,060 tons of general and refrigerated cargo on board. Along with her sisterships, *Corinthic* and *Athenic*, the *Ionic* was specifically designed for White Star Line's longstanding trade to the Southern Hemisphere. Each of the liners had accommodation for 121 first-class, 117 second-class, and 450 third-class passengers, as well as considerable cargo space. In 1932 the *Ionic*'s passenger accommodation was altered to tourist class only. On the voyage featured here the vessel is listed under the management of Shaw, Savill & Albion, which had passed into the control of the White Star group in 1910. Although the color schemes of both companies were almost identical, differing only in the color of the stripe around the hull and the shade of the funnel, White Star vessels traditionally had white crow's nests, which the *Ionic* carries in this picture. A year later, when White Star merged with Cunard Line, the twin-screw liner was sold to Shaw, Savill & Albion, who continued to operate the ship in New Zealand service, but painted the crows-nest in its own color scheme. In January of 1937 the *Ionic* made its final voyage from England to Osaka, Japan, where it was broken up for scrap. The *Corinthic* had been broken up five years previously, but the *Athenic* survived until 1962, having been converted to a whaling ship as early as 1928.

Stella Polaris

Looking like a massive private yacht, the cruise liner *Stella Polaris* glides through Gaillard Cut on 27 January 1934 during a world cruise from New York to Monaco. At the time, the white-hulled vessel was the world's largest motor-driven ship designed exclusively for cruising. Owned by the Bergen Steamship Company of Norway, the *Stella Polaris* had been completed in 1927 at the Götaverken yard, Göteborg, Sweden, for a cost of 4 million Swedish kroner. Her original tonnage under Bergen ownership was 5,057 gross and 2,747 net, with an overall length of 416 feet 1 inch and a breadth of 50 feet 8 inches. Her main machinery consisted of two Götaverken-built B&W diesel engines yielding a total of 3,200 brake horsepower (BHP) and driving twin screws. The yachtlike appearance of the *Stella Polaris*, which incorporated two tall masts, a bowsprit, and counter stern, made her a most attractive vessel and a favorite of the wealthy. Accommodation in spacious cabins was limited to 190 passengers. During World War II, the *Stella Polaris* was used for several years as a barracks ship for German U-Boat crews in northern Norway. After the war, the cruise liner was completely reconditioned by her builders and again entered commercial cruise service in late 1946. Five years later the *Stella Polaris* was sold to Rederi A/B Clipper of Malmo, Sweden, who operated the ship under her original name until 1969. At the age of 42, the vessel was sold to Japanese interests for use as a floating hotel in northern Japan. Renamed *Scandinavia*, the ship is reported still to be afloat in this capacity.

Corsair

Pleasure craft of the affluent and famous have always been frequent visitors to Panama. One such vessel was J.P. Morgan's yacht *Corsair*, photographed transiting northbound at Gamboa on 31 January 1934. This was the fourth Morgan-owned *Corsair*, the first having been purchased secondhand in 1882, while the second and third followed as new-built ships in 1890 and 1899. *Corsair* (IV) was designed by H.J. Gielow and built for $2.5 million by Bath Iron Works in 1930. It was to be one of the last of the big steam-powered luxury yachts, as most builders thereafter shifted to diesel propulsion. The 2,653-ton *Corsair* was returning to the United States after a trip out to the Galápagos Islands. The ship had passed through Panama southbound only nine days earlier. E.F. Hutton's yacht *Hussar* had preceded the *Corsair* through Panama on January 11th. Five days earlier, on January 6th, A. D. Chandler's *Blue Dolphin 1* had transited from the Galápagos bound for Gloucester. The *Blue Dolfin*'s northbound transit was followed by that of H. Trumbull's yacht *Audacious*, which passed through Panama on January 29th during a voyage from San Francisco to the Caribbean. One can only wonder if business was mixed with pleasure on these interocean outings. The *Corsair* was laid up the following year and eventually came under the command of the British during World War II. After the war, the ship was fitted out for luxury cruising on the U.S. Pacific Coast, but was wrecked off Acapulco, Mexico, on 12 November 1949.

Pennsylvania

On 5 March 1934, the 18,200-ton turbo-electric liner *Pennsylvania* transited from San Francisco to New York with several hundred passengers and 6,731 tons of general cargo on board. The ship, along with her two sisters, the *Virginia* and *California*, had been built by Newport News Shipbuilding & Drydock for the intercoastal services of the Panama-Pacific Line. The three twin-screw liners were the largest commercial vessels to have been built in the United States and cost their owner, American Line, over 21 million dollars. They were also the largest electrically propelled commercial vessels afloat. The *California* was the first of the sisters to arrive at Panama, passing through on her way from New York to San Francisco on 3 February 1928 with 639 passengers aboard. Registering 11,935 U.S. net tons, the liner paid tolls of $14,918.75. The *Virginia*, launched on 18 October 1928, made its maiden transit of the canal on December 14th of that year, followed by the *Pennsylvania* five weeks later. In 1937 the three liners were turned over to the U.S. Maritime Commission and rebuilt for the South American service of the American Republic Line (Moore & McCormack) as the *Uruguay, Brazil,* and *Argentina*. This work resulted in reduced passenger accommodation, increased cargo capacity, and the elimination of one funnel per ship. After war duty as military transports, the vessels were again overhauled and placed back into commercial service in 1947. With the introduction of new tonnage for Moore-McCormack routes during the late 1950s, all three liners were laid up and then sold for scrap in 1963.

170

Bremen

On 15 February 1939 the Panama Canal welcomed a leviathan, the 51,731 gross-registered-ton *Bremen* of North German Lloyd. Launched in 1928, the ship was the pride of the German merchant fleet, having won the Blue Riband on her maiden Atlantic crossing in 1929 with a speed of 27.83 knots. The liner's transit of the Panama Canal, undertaken while the ship was on a winter cruise out of New York, cost her owners $15,143.40 and established the *Bremen* as the largest passenger vessel to have transited to that date, a record she kept for many years. In this photograph, the ship's tremendous size is made more apparent by the empty adjacent locks, which were being overhauled. In their depth, men can be seen working around the 600-ton lock gates. Also visible are the subterranean culvert portals, each four and a half feet wide, through which water enters and exits the locks. The *Bremen* continued on her cruise, arriving back at New York for what was to be her last visit in late August. Though held up briefly by U.S. authorities, the large liner was able to sail for Europe on August 30th. A few days later Germany invaded Poland. Altering course to the north, the *Bremen* escaped patrolling British warships and entered the Russian port of Murmansk on September 6th. Three months later the ship sailed on to Bremerhaven. Though plans were laid to outfit the *Bremen* as a troop transport for the expected invasion of England, the liner was instead turned into an accommodation ship. In March of 1941, while being used in this capacity, an accidental fire completely destroyed the vessel. The wreck was later broken up for scrap.

4

Cargo Ships and Work Craft

The cargo ship was destined to be the principal user and financial supporter of the Panama Canal, and the canal was to reciprocate by opening up new and lucrative areas of trade for such working vessels. With the first official transits completed on 15 August 1914, the initial vessels through were neither battleships nor luxury liners but common cargo carriers. An American freighter, the 1903-built *Arizonan* of the American-Hawaiian Line, followed the historic southbound transit of the *Ancon* by just a few hours. On the following day, the *Pleiades*, a cargo vessel of the Luckenback Steamship Company, made the first commercial northbound transit. Thereafter, cargo vessels swarmed to the isthmus, leaving facilities and businesses on the Strait of Magellan to stagnate.

For American shipping, Seattle was suddenly 7,800 miles nearer to New York, and San Francisco 8,800 miles closer to New Orleans. On international routes, the steaming distance between Guayaquil and New York was cut by over 7,000 miles, and Melbourne was brought 1,300 miles closer to Liverpool. When the *Arizonan* returned through the canal in November of 1914,

en route from San Francisco to New York, a calculation was made to determine what savings the Panama Canal afforded over the Strait of Magellan route. Even with a week's delay at Panama caused by a minor earth slide, it was calculated that the ship's owners were saved over $1,000 by the new waterway. This figure was arrived at on the basis of a stated operating cost of $450 a day for the 8,672-ton vessel. The canal route saved 19.8 days over the Magellan route, or $8,910. After deducting the $7,891 in tolls charged by the canal, a savings of $1,019 was realized.

The opening of the Panama Canal caught world commercial shipping in transition. The age of steam had arrived, but sailing ships were still hauling paying cargoes on the high seas, and diesel-driven motorships were just starting to make their appearance. For sailing ships the canal was to prove a difficult time-saver, and only a few made use of it. Between the opening date of 15 August 1914 and 1 September 1916, 33 such vessels crossed the isthmus, eight of which were in ballast. The sailing ships amounted to only 1.47 percent of total transits, represented .65 percent of the total transited

To be sunk in May of 1942, the Texas Company's tanker *New Jersey* transits Pedro Miguel Locks on 12 November 1931 in company with the American-Hawaiian freighter *Minnesotan*.

net tonnage, and carried a meager .75 percent of the total cargo. They ranged in size from small schooners like the *Bertha E. May*, 50 net tons, to the four-masted steel bark *Daylight*, 3,599 net tons, one of the largest sailing ships in the world.

In this same time frame, 40 motorships used the canal, 24 passing south into the Pacific and 16 transiting north to the Atlantic. The first motorship transit was undertaken by Johnson Line's *Kronprinzessin Margareta*, which had sailed outbound for South American Pacific coast ports via the Strait of Magellan and returned homeward via the Panama Canal on 18 October 1914. She was followed a month later by East Asiatic Company's *Jutlandia*, which made the first southbound motorship transit of the waterway on 20 November 1914. Between 15 August 1914 and 1 September 1916, motor vessels accounted for 1.84 percent of all transits, represented 2.3227 percent of total net tonnage transited, and carried 2.3233 percent of all water-bound cargo across the isthmus.

Transits of the canal by sailing ships dwindled rapidly after the peak year for sailing traffic, 1918, during which 73 transits were made—55 by French vessels. In the first nine months of 1924, only four wind-driven vessels used the waterway. Two of these were under the flag of Finland, one of Norway, and one of Peru. One of the Finnish vessels carried a cargo of nitrates from Chile to France, and the other three carried guano from the west coast of Peru to the United States. On 24 May 1932, the Swedish sailing ship *C.B. Pedersen* arrived at Balboa en route from Melbourne, Australia, to Cobh,

Ireland, with a cargo of 2,960 tons of wheat. Built in Italy in 1891, the 289-foot Swedish vessel was to be one of the last commerical sailing ships to transit Panama with a paying cargo. Only a few months earlier, on 12 January 1932, the last American-flag commercial sailing ship, the *Tusitala*, had made her final transit at the end of a tow line after having been becalmed off the coast of Costa Rica.

Eventually, motorships were to become commonplace at the canal. The revolutionary vessels had several advantages over coal-driven steamers of the day. They could bunker the whole supply of fuel oil needed for a long trip at one place, whereas the steamers were forced to call at extra ports for bunkering purposes. They could carry their oil supply in their double bottom, so that cargo space equivalent to the bulk of the coal-boxes in the steamers was saved, and the engine crew of the motor vessel could be reduced to half that of the coal steamer. The principal disadvantage of the motorship was the high cost of fuel oil compared to the price of coal. On the route between Europe and the west coast of North America, however, fuel oil could be picked up cheaply at California ports. In a very short time, this route became one of the world's leading motorship routes.

While Ernest Hallen recorded the last of the sailing ships and the first of the motorships at Panama, the vast majority of his cargo-vessel photographs were of the common steamers, a tragic number of which would earn but a simple epitaph in the coming destruction wrought by World War II.

Corozal

High and dry for a routine scraping of her hull, the Panama Canal dredge *Corozal* lies beached on Naos Island during the summer of 1912. Built in 1911 by William Simons & Company, Ltd., Renfrew, Scotland, the *Corozal*'s delivery voyage to Panama's west coast was one of the longest trips ever undertaken by a fully assembled ladder dredge. Sailing from Renfrew on 1 December 1911, the *Corozal* journeyed by way of Funchal, Montevideo, and the Magellan Strait for Balboa, arriving at the Pacific port on 27 March 1912. On completion of this trip the vessel's log showed a total voyage duration of 117 days and 12,064 miles. Built at a cost of $399,340.00, the *Corozal* was given a number of tests before being allowed to sail for her work site. These included the excavation of several types of materials at various depths, most of the work being carried out in Belfast Harbor. During these trials the *Corozal* managed to excavate 1,114 tons of material in 41 minutes at depths ranging from 40 to 50 feet, at a rate of 1,482 cubic yards an hour. In the last load an actual dredging depth of 53 feet 2 inches below the surface was reached. The *Corozal* played an important role in the clearing of the Pacific entrance channel from Balboa to Miraflores Locks, work that required the removal of approximately four million cubic yards of spoil. In 1919, after the completion of canal and slide excavation work, the *Corozal* was sold to the United States Engineering Office and left the isthmus for Philadelphia under tow of the Navy collier *Vulcan* on 11 December 1919.

180

Salvor and *Newport*

Shortly after midnight on 17 August 1912, a 185-foot section of wharf at Balboa collapsed, sinking the Pacific Mail steamship *Newport* moored alongside. Fortunately, a nearby policeman heard the structure start to give way and warned crewmembers, who were consequently able to scramble to safety. The *Newport* was loaded with approximately 1,500 tons of general cargo at the time and had been scheduled to get under way for Mexican and Central American ports on the 19th. The 2,735-ton cargo/passenger ship, built in 1880 by J. Roach & Sons, was brought back to the surface by the Canadian salvage vessel *Salvor*, which began work on September 9th and had the vessel raised by November 10th. The *Newport*'s cargo was dried out and later put up for sale at the American wharf in Panama City. Interested buyers were able to rummage through a wide variety of items, including rope, wire, cloth, medical supplies, liquors, machetes, ironwork, cloth, lamps, and crockery. Much of the steamship's cargo was purchased in block by the Chicago House Wrecking Company, which was in the process of salvaging equipment brought to Panama by the French Canal Company. The *Newport* was repaired after her mishap and lived on to make many more runs through the Panama Canal, eventually being abandoned at San Francisco in 1933. The *Salvor*, built in 1869 as the *Danube*, sailed for her home base of Victoria, B.C., on November 19th. Eight years later the 887-ton salvage vessel was sold to Spanish interests and renamed *Nervion*. The ship disappeared from Lloyds Register under this name in 1931/32.

Jutlandia

The first motorship to pass through the Panama Canal southbound, the Danish-flag *Jutlandia*, transited on 20 November 1914 with 2,000 tons of general cargo for North American Pacific Coast ports. This photograph shows the 4,874-ton freighter on 16 January 1915 during her return voyage with 6,500 tons of cargo on board. At this point of her transit, the ship is being towed past the disastrous Cucaracha Slide, which had come down on October 14th of the preceding year. The *Jutlandia*, owned by Akties. Det. Ostasiatiske Kompagni, Copenhagen, and built by Barclay, Curle & Co. Ltd., Glasgow, was the first large diesel-driven cargo vessel constructed in the United Kingdom. She was equipped with two eight-cylinder, four-stroke diesel engines of 2,500 horsepower manufactured by Burmeister and Wain of Copenhagen. The early motorships, particularly those ordered for Scandinavian owners, were easily identified by their lack of a distinctive funnel. Exhaust gases were discharged through a slender stack, that of the *Jutlandia* being visible here almost in line with the vessel's main mast. In 1934, after 22 years of service under the Danish flag, the *Jutlandia* was sold to Carriso Inc., Panama, and renamed *Noumea*. Three years later the historic vessel again changed hands, this time going to the Danmotor Shipping Co., Panama, as *Dan*. Within a few months of this transaction the ship stranded at Gisslan on 16 December 1937 while on a passage from Hull to Ratso. Though refloated, the 25-year-old ship was found uneconomical to repair and was sold for scrap.

184

John Ena

The first commercial sailing ship to use the Panama Canal in both directions was the small, 335-ton three-masted schooner *Zeta*, owned by Robert Wilcox, but the first large sailing vessel transit was undertaken by the 2,842-ton four-masted bark *John Ena*. The vessel passed southbound on 22 January 1915 with a cargo of 11,686 cases of refined petroleum and 306 barrels of wax destined for Kobe, Japan. With canal measurements of 2,609 tons, the *John Ena* paid a transit charge of $3,130.80 and a towing fee of $302.15. This photograph shows the ship as she was towed past the infamous Gold Hill slide. Note the lady in white, quite probably the captain's wife, standing on the raised poop deck aft. Built by R. Duncan & Co. Ltd., Pt. Glasgow, in 1892, the *John Ena* was owned by the San Francisco Shipping Co. Ltd. and managed by the firm of A.P. Lorentzen at the time this transit was made. A year later the ship was sold to Rolph Navigation & Coal Company for $180,000, then resold to the Standard Oil Company of California. Her next owner of record was Robert Dollar & Co., under whose flag the ship sailed to the west coast in 1921. Following a period of lay-up, the *John Ena* was sent through Panama to New York with a cargo of lumber in 1925. On her return trip in early 1926, the ship made a short call at Cristóbal to load 223 tons of cargo; then she proceeded on to California ports for discharge. The steel-hulled vessel was finally broken up for scrap at Los Angeles in 1934/35.

Saint Andre

On 16 March 1915 the first French vessel to use the Panama Canal, the 5,765-ton *Saint Andre*, transited north from New Caledonia and Tahiti to Glasgow with a cargo of 6,800 tons of chrome ore. There were no celebrations to record the event, but there was a great amount of respect exhibited along the canal for the nation that had accomplished so much at Panama. Although the French had been defeated in their attempt to build an interocean canal between the Atlantic and the Pacific, much of their work had been incorporated into the American project. The line of the proposed French canal had been much the same as that of the American route, thus 29,908,000 of the 78,146,960 cubic yards excavated by the French were useful in the American effort. In addition, the French had provided surveys, borings, and hydrographic records, as well as two hospitals, a number of shops and residential villages, and considerable railroad and excavating equipment, all purchased by the Americans on 4 May 1904. Oddly, once the waterway was completed, the French merchant marine made little use of it. In 1915 only three French vessels transited. In the following year only one. Even in 1921, when 2,791 ships passed across the isthmus, only 44 flew the French flag. The *Saint Andre*, shown at Pedro Miguel Locks, was built at St.Nazaire in 1912, operated by La Compagnie Navale de L'Océanie, and eventually sold to Italian shipbreakers at Genoa, Italy, in 1936. Of interest in this photograph is the clearance provided for towing locomotives and lock personnel under the grid-like "emergency dam" at the left.

Janna

On 25 March 1915 the 1,612-ton Norwegian bark *Janna* became the first large sailing ship to transit the Panama Canal northbound. Built in 1896 by A. Rodger, Glasgow, the *Janna* was bound from San Francisco to Bergen with 2,631 tons of barley on board. Because of World War I, the ship was well marked with her country of registration (Norge) and national colors. While this precaution safely saw her through the hostilities, it did not guard the vessel against perils of the sea. In September of 1922 the three-masted sailing ship was posted missing after having departed Sydney, Australia, for England on 3 December 1921. Sailing vessels, such as the *Janna*, were not regular callers at Panama. In the canal's first two years of operation, only 33 such vessels transited, 14 from the Atlantic and 19 from the Pacific. Eight of these ships were in ballast. The Isthmus of Panama, though easy to reach by steam, was somewhat more difficult to arrive at by sail. Owners of sailing ships, therefore, had to ensure that the savings in time afforded by the new waterway would offset transit charges. A case in point was that of the small barkentine *John C. Meyer* that followed *Janna* down the coast. It took the *Meyer* two months and a day to reach Balboa on a voyage from Portland, Oregon, to Quebec, Canada. Calculating a total voyage time of 100 days via Panama compared to about 150 days via Cape Horn, the shipowner's expenses on the *Meyer* had to be under $22.85 a day to justify avoiding the canal and its $1,142.50 transit charge.

190

Lord Templetown

Dredges pause at Culebra Cut as the sailing ship *Lord Templetown* transits south-bound on 12 June 1915 with the assistance of a canal tug. The vessel was making its maiden voyage through the waterway while on a trip from Leith to San Francisco with 3,293 tons of coke on board. Behind the sailing vessel is the Norwegian steamship *Torsdale*, which was transiting in ballast from Cardiff to Antofagasta, Chile. A large vessel, the *Lord Templetown* had been built by Harland & Wolff, Belfast, in 1886 as a full-rigged ship of 2,152-tons. Later cut down to a three-masted barque, the vessel passed into Canadian ownership during the early 1900s and was placed under the management of Eschen and Minor of San Francisco. During World War I, the steel-hulled ship came under the American flag and was a frequent caller along the North American west coast. In 1921 after arriving at San Francisco from Chile with a cargo of nitrate on board, the *Lord Templetown* was laid up. In 1925 the 39-year-old sailing ship was towed north to Seattle by Coastwise Steamship & Barge and rigged down for use as an ore and log carrier. In this unglamorous employment she joined many other sailing vessels of the period that could no longer compete with steam and motor-driven ships. It was not until 1957 that the hulk of the *Lord Templetown* was finally broken up for scrap at Portland, Oregon. Several of the sailing ship's fittings are on display at the San Francisco Maritime Museum, and one of her anchors can still be seen in Vanier Park, Vancouver, British Columbia.

Strathearn

In August of 1916 the Glasgow-registered steamer *Strathearn* became the first merchant vessel to use the newly completed dry dock at Balboa. The dock had been built to the same dimensions as the Panama Canal locks, 1,000 feet by 110 feet. Hence, the 4,419-ton *Strathearn*, measuring 370 feet by 52 feet, was easily accommodated. The 1906-built steamer had been on a voyage from Pensacola, Florida, to Pisagua, Chile, in ballast when she called at the Balboa facility for replacement of her rudder pin bushings. This view, taken on 25 August 1916, shows the amount of tumble-home, or inward inclination of the upward portion of the hull, that was commonly built into many ships of that period. Workers have erected scaffolding around the cargo vessel, using cables rigged over the side. Towards the stern, supports have been used to surround the rudder assembly. Beyond the dry dock the extensive workshops of Balboa can be seen. The *Strathearn*, which was owned by the Strathearn Steam Ship Company and managed by Burrell & Sons, was sold to the Anglo-American Oil Company four years after this picture was taken. In 1923 the vessel passed into Greek ownership, undergoing several name changes before being sold to Italian interests in 1939. While trading as the *Moscardin*, the freighter was seized by the British government at Newcastle-upon-Tyne during World War II. Renamed *Empire Gunner*, the 35-year-old vessel was bombed and sunk by German aircraft off the coast of England on 7 September 1941.

194

USFS *Roosevelt*

A small but historic ship, the *Roosevelt* was launched on 24 March 1905 at Bucksport, Maine, for the Arctic expeditions of Admiral Robert E. Peary. It was the first ship built in the Western Hemisphere for such northern ventures and had one of the strongest hulls ever constructed of wood. In some places the sides of the ship were 30 inches thick. The 614-ton vessel served Peary well. In April 1909 the explorer was able to reach the North Pole overland after sailing the *Roosevelt* to within 420 miles of his goal. In September of that year, the stout ship sailed back into New York Harbor flying the North Pole flag, "a flag which never before had entered any port in history." Peary did not return to the Arctic, but his sturdy ship did. Refitted for work under the U.S. Bureau of Fisheries, the *Roosevelt* transited from the Atlantic to the Pacific in 1917, stopping at Balboa for repairs—and this photograph—in March of that year. After reaching Seattle on 23 April 1917, the vessel took up surveillance operations in the Pribilof Islands, rescuing several ice-bound vessels in 1918. A year later, in deteriorating condition, the ship was sold. She emerged in 1923 as a tug under private ownership. In January of 1937, while towing a hulk to New York, the *Roosevelt* was forced back into Cristóbal by heavy weather. Badly damaged and leaking, the little explorer was driven ashore and abandoned on the mud flats, where her wooden hull eventually rotted away.

Batsford

Whenever dredging work was to be undertaken in the main channel of the Panama Canal, ships were transited in convoys. This was quite frequent in the first few years of the waterway's operation, especially in the slide-prone Gaillard Cut area. This 1917 photograph captures such a convoy being guided northbound by the British freighter *Batsford*, which was proceeding under tow. The *Batsford*, owned at the time by Century Shipping, was on a voyage from Antofagasta, Chile, to Colón for orders. Her cargo consisted of 7,900 tons of nitrate. Two other ships in the convoy, the Dutch *Venbergen* and British *Lady Sybil*, also carried nitrate cargos. The mineral was much in demand during World War I and remained the leading northbound cargo through Panama for many years. Over 7,464,860 tons of the commodity were transported across the isthmus in the first five years of canal operation. This represented slightly over one-quarter of all cargoes transited. In this same period, British ships were the most frequent users of the canal. Of 450 vessels that transited in the first half of fiscal 1917, 208 were British. From the beginning of canal operations on 15 August 1914 until the beginning of 1917, British-flag vessels accounted for 45 percent of all transits, or 1,253 ships. The *Batsford*, launched in 1913 by J.L. Thompson & Sons, Sutherland, was sold to Canadian Pacific in 1918, then resold three more times before becoming the *Tozan Maru* in 1937. Seven months after passing to the Japanese flag, the ship was wrecked on Goto Island in the East China Sea while on a passage from Yawata to Keelung.

Diria

This view, taken in June of 1918, shows the wide assortment of craft that made use of the Cristóbal repair facilities located near Mt. Hope. The photograph appears to have been taken from the stern of a ship that was in the dry dock. On the wharf in the foreground, several spectators, some seated on a dredge boom, take in the photographer's efforts with mild interest. Berthed alongside the wharf is a small American submarine, partially shaded by a canvas awning. Behind the submarine are two local vessels, a Panamanian sailing craft and the steam-powered *Rey Del Rio*. Behind the *Rey Del Rio* is the slightly larger Colombia-registered *Balboa* and an unidentified canal tug. To the right side of the picture is the large canal tug *Porto Bello* and the five-masted sailing ship *Diria*. The *Porto Bello* had been built at Baltimore in 1906 as the *Robert H. Smith* and was purchased in 1907 by the Isthmian Canal Commission from the American Towing and Lightering Company. After many years of service in Panama, the tug was sold in 1929 to the Reichert Towing Line, Inc., of Brooklyn, New York. The *Diria*, an auxiliary five-masted schooner, had been built in 1917 by the Columbia Engineering Works at Portland, Oregon. One year after this photograph was taken, the sailing ship foundered off the coast of Cuba, fortunately without loss of life. In the far background, the hulk of an unidentified steamer can be seen, seemingly burnt-out and beached in shallow water.

Eten

On 13 April 1919 the *Eten*, formerly the 1907-built German steamship *Rhakotis*, transited northbound for New York from Balboa, where she had undergone extensive reconditioning in the Panama Canal shops. She carries three anchors in this photograph. One is an older model unchained in its starboard deck mount. Along with a number of other German vessels, the *Rhakotis* had been interned by Peru during World War I. Following an agreement between the governments of Peru and the United States, several of the larger ships were towed to Panama in late 1918 to be rebuilt for operation by the United States Shipping Board. The *Rhakotis* and the liner *Sierra Cordoba* left Callao on 6 September 1918 in tow of the Panama Canal dredge *Culebra*. Three other German vessels, the *Luxor, Uarda,* and *Anubis,* followed at a later date. All five ships were taken to the Panama Canal shipyard at Balboa where they were repaired and placed back in commission over a period of six months. Other German vessels interned at Chilean ports were towed back through the canal by British tugs. These included the *Riol*, under tow of *St. Ewe,* the *Abessinia,* towed by the *St. Botolph*, and from Iquique, the *Holstein*, brought north by the *St. Blasey.* German sailors were taken south in the steamer *Lucie Woerman* to return a number of stranded German sailing ships. After several years of U.S. government service, the *Eten* was eventually returned to Peru to become part of that country's national fleet as the *Rimac*. This employment lasted a further 37 years. The ship was finally sold for scrap in Japan during 1959.

San Joaquin

Taken from an unusual vantage point in Gaillard Cut, this 27 December 1919 photograph shows the Norwegian tanker *San Joaquin* transiting in ballast from Iquique, Chile, to Tampico, Mexico. The master, pilot, and helmsman can be made out on the vessel's sparse navigation bridge. Two of the crew are using the tanker's bridge-like "catwalk" to cross between the forecastle and the pilothouse superstructure. One gentleman has taken up a viewing point situated right forward on the ship's bow. Though owned by Akties Tankfart (W.Wilhelmsen) of Tonsberg, Norway, a white "U" on the *San Joaquin*'s funnel denotes that she was probably under long-term charter to the Union Oil Company. At this time a number of American oil companies were chartering Norwegian-owned tonnage for international petroleum movements. Union had four such chartered Norwegian ships in operation between the Mexican oil fields and South America. By 1921 their constant shuttling through the canal comprised over a third of all Norwegian-flag transits for the year, with three of the tankers crossing the isthmus 15 times. Built in 1913 by the British firm of Sir J. Laing & Sons, Ltd., Sunderland, the *San Joaquin* became the *Melville* in 1929. Six years later she was sold to Greek interests and was renamed *Iolcos*. In 1937 the London firm of Finchley S.S. Co. Ltd. purchased the ship and renamed her *Woodford*. A few months later, on 1 September 1937, the vessel was torpedoed and sunk during the Spanish Civil War while on a voyage from the Romanian oil fields to Valencia.

Belen Quezada

Though the Panama Canal runs through the Republic of Panama, few Panamanian ships were to be seen in the waterway during its early years of operation. Those that did transit were usually small vessels involved in the intercoastal trades, the motor schooner *Belen Quezada* being a good example. Shown at Miraflores on 10 January 1920, the *Belen Quezada* was on a voyage from Port Angeles, Washington, to Antilla, Cuba, with 850 tons of lumber on board. In the same year that the *Belen Quezada* made her transit, a Spanish shipping company, Sota Y Aznar of Bilbao, sought to register a portion of its fleet in the Republic of Panama. At the time, Panama had no laws to cover such a move, the existing regulations providing only for the coastal trades. By an executive decree dated 7 October 1921, the president of Panama ruled that the vessels of Sota Y Aznar might be admitted to register under the Panamanian flag. The ships became subject to an annual tax of 10 cents per net registered ton and a registration fee of $1 per net ton, rates highly advantageous to the Spanish company. Sota Y Aznar's move to Panama's flag was, in time, followed by many other shipping companies seeking the republic's lenient shipping taxes. In 1915, the first full year of canal operation, only two small Panamanian ships transited the canal. By 1932 this number had grown to 102 ships. In recent years Panamanian-registered ships transiting the canal have exceeded those of any other flag.

Ceylon Maru

Japan was a growing power in the Pacific, both militarily and commercially, when this photograph of the *Ceylon Maru* in Pedro Miguel Locks was taken on 13 June 1920. The ship was on a voyage from New York to Kobe with 4,702 tons of general cargo on board. Behind the freighter looms a large American battleship, quite probably the USS *South Carolina*, which was transiting in company with the USS *Michigan* on that day. The 1904-built *Ceylon Maru* carries old-fashioned stocked anchors, both of which are at the ready, but otherwise is well maintained, a hallmark of Japanese liner ships of the period. Owned by Nippon Yusen Kabushiki Kaisha (N.Y.K. Line), the 4,897-ton freighter was one of 118 Japanese vessels to transit the canal in 1920. This represented a steady increase from 1915, when only six Japanese ships used the waterway. The vast majority of Japanese commercial vessels transited Panama from the Atlantic to the Pacific, a predominance of nearly 2 to 1. Most Japanese ships sailed outbound via Suez, bringing cargo home through Panama from Europe and U.S. Atlantic/Gulf ports. An important commodity on this route was silk. In the early 1930s, N.Y.K. Line introduced six new 18-knot motorships specifically designed to transport this high-value product. Older vessels, such as the *Ceylon Maru*, were displaced to less important trades. On 27 February 1944 the *Ceylon Maru* was torpedoed and sunk by American submarine USS *Grayback* some 100 nautical miles south of Nagasaki, Japan.

208

Irene S. Wilkinson

Although sailing ships were not frequent users of the Panama Canal, even more rare were wooden-hulled sailing ships. Such was the four-masted sailing vessel *Irene S. Wilkinson*, shown in this undated photograph approaching Pedro Miguel Locks with the assistance of a canal tug. The *Irene S. Wilkinson* had been built by the Georgia Shipbuilding Company of Savannah, Georgia, in 1918 and measured 179 by 38 feet with a 16-foot draft. Operated for the owner's own account, the 818-ton sailing ship made a number of transits through the canal between 1918 and 1924 with timber cargoes on board, most of which were destined for furniture and piano manufacturers in the United States. On this voyage a cargo of Central American hardwood logs, just visible under the ship's built-up wooden working platform, is being transported through the canal. The vessel made at least one trip as far south as the River Plate on the east coast of South America in 1919. In April 1924 the *Wilkinson* returned to Panama for repairs. A large amount of rotten planking was removed from her hull, and the entire bottom of the ship was cemented. Shortly after this work, the vessel was sold to the Howard Lumber Co. of Alexandria, Virginia. In 1929 the ship changed hands again, this time going to Fred G. Viles of Jacksonville, Florida. Her final owner of record was the company of Fielder & Mitchess of Tampa, Florida, who last operated the ship in 1933. Thereafter, she disappeared from international shipping registers and is presumed to have been abandoned or broken up.

Sussex

Not all intended transits of the Panama Canal took place without incident. At 10:25 P.M. on 3 January 1921, the 6,930-ton British freighter *Sussex* grounded on Limon Bay Breakwater while approaching Cristóbal Harbor without the aid of a pilot. The vessel had left St. John's, New Brunswick, several weeks earlier and was proceeding to New Zealand ports with over 11,000 tons of cargo on board. This photograph, taken the morning after the grounding, shows the vessel flying its distress flags, while several of its crew survey their plight. The *Sussex* was eventually pulled off the rocks on January 11th by the canal salvage vessel *Favorite*, but only after 1,700 tons of cargo had been discharged into lighters from the freighter's two forward holds. In this picture the *Favorite* is visible just astern of the *Sussex*, and assisting tugs *Gorgona* and *Tavernilla* lie beyond the field of view. After an underwater inspection, the cargo ship was taken through the canal under tow and placed in Balboa Dry Dock on January 26th for repairs. Damage was found to extend from the ships forepeak to the center of Hatch No. 1, necessitating the replacement of 36 plates and the forging of a new stem piece. The vessel's owners, the Federal Steam Navigation Company, elected to complete survey work at the same time, thus delaying the steamer's completion until February 21st. The *Sussex* then reloaded her cargo and continued to New Zealand. The 1900-built ship remained a frequent visitor to the canal until 1929, when she was sold for scrap in Japan.

Nashaba

Drawing 26 feet of water, and with both anchors dipped the American freighter *Nashaba* is shown transiting from Portland, Oregon, to Limerick, Ireland, with 7,612 tons of wheat flour on board. The 6,062-ton cargo ship had been completed only a few months earlier by the Pacific Coast Shipbuilding Company at Bay Point, California. Like many other American commercial vessels of the period, the *Nashaba*'s design was one of several adopted and overseen by the U.S. Emergency Fleet Corporation, which had been established during World War I. Though upright and boxy in appearance from broadside, the standard design ships did have their curves, as is evident in this bow view of the *Nashaba* taken at Pedro Miguel Locks on 10 September 1921. At the time of this transit, the *Nashaba* was being operated by the firm of McCormick & McPherson and was one of a large number of American vessels engaged in the grain and flour trade between North American west-coast ports and Europe. Grain and flour rivaled nitrate as the leading eastbound commodity through Panama during the immediate post–World War I years. In 1933 the *Nashaba* was sold by the United States Shipping Board to Lykes Bros. of New Orleans and was operated for several years by that firm's Ripley Steamship Company. On 26 February 1945 while proceeding in convoy from Cardiff to Ghent with military supplies on board, the *Nashaba* contacted a mine that exploded near the ship's number 4 hold. The freighter sank in shallow water with the loss of two men.

214

Orient City

Representative of a British tramp freighter of the period, the 4,218-ton *Orient City* waits in the west chamber of Pedro Miguel Locks on 15 September 1921 while transiting in ballast from Newcastle, England, to Portland, Oregon. Behind the cargo ship are the Panama Canal tug *La Boca* and U.S. Army mine planter *General W.M. Graham*, both transiting to Balboa. The *Orient City* had been built in 1911 by Richardson Duck & Co., Stockton, as the *Cloughton*. After service in the London & Northern Steamship Company fleet, the vessel was purchased by St. Just S.S. Co. Ltd. and placed under the management of W.R. Smith & Sons Ltd. In the freighter's rigging can be seen the numeral pendant "1," denoting her transit as the first southbound movement of the day. The initial "S," a traditional hallmark of Sir William Reardon Smith & Sons Ltd., is partially visible on the *Orient City*'s funnel. Reardon Smith vessels were not frequent users of the Panama Canal, but the rapid buildup of Pacific Coast-Europe grain traffic in 1921 brought several of the company's ships through the waterway. In August of 1921 fully one-third of the ships crossing the isthmus from the Atlantic to the Pacific were bound for ports on the west coast of the United States and Canada to load grain. British ships accounted for 970 of the 2,892 ship transits recorded in 1921, moving 3,721,932 tons of cargo across the isthmus and paying tolls amounting to $3,976,395. The *Orient City* made several of these voyages. In 1935, after 24 years of service, the freighter was sold to Italian shipbreakers for scrap.

Cacique

One of many Grace Line ships that regularly passed through the Panama Canal, the 6,202-ton *Cacique* was built in 1910 by Short Bros. Ltd., Sunderland, in the United Kingdom. The vessel is shown leaving Pedro Miguel Locks on 16 September 1921, bound from Chile for New York with 4,600 tons of nitrate and ore aboard. W.R. Grace & Company, owner of the *Cacique*, had been formed by William Russell Grace in 1865. Grace had gone out to Peru with his father in 1850 and, as a teenager, had become involved in the successful export of guano from Peru's offshore islands. By combining forces with his two brothers, Michael and John, and joining in a partnership with John and Francis Bryce of England, Grace quickly built up a trading empire in South America. In 1884 the company began an irregular steamship service between New York and Valparaiso via the Strait of Magellan. Speculating that there would be a dramatic increase in South American trade once the Panama Canal was completed, the firm ordered more vessels in 1910/1912. This put the trading concern in a good position to obtain high charter rates for its ships during and immediately after World War I. In the years 1916/1920 the Grace Line made almost $27,000,000 in gross profits. Thereafter, as the trading fleets of other companies were rebuilt and a world depression took hold, profits fell off rapidly, averaging only $400,000 annually from 1928 to 1934. The *Cacique* was sold for scrap during the later portion of this period, arriving at Yokohama on 12 March 1934.

Cedar Branch

Built in 1910 by Bartram & Sons, Sunderland, the 3,554-ton cargo ship *Cedar Branch* carries a bowsprit and figurehead, characteristic of the days of sail. The ship is seen on 16 September 1921 proceeding southbound on a voyage from London to Guayaquil with 1,092 tons of general cargo on board. Owned by the Nautilus Steam Ship Company, the *Cedar Branch* was one of several vessels managed by F&W Ritson that ran between the United Kingdom and the west coast of South America. Shortly after the canal was opened, the Nautilus ships would sail outbound through the Strait of Magellan and return home via Panama. Later, most ships used the canal in both directions. The usual homebound cargo was nitrate, but another Nautilus vessel, the *Lime Branch*, returned to England in April of 1921 carrying, amongst other cargo, two cases of ambergris, seven barrels of sperm whale teeth, and one-half ton of gold and silver. In the year this photograph was taken, 970 British-flagged vessels, totaling 5,035,686 grt, passed through the canal. This represented 32 percent of total traffic and $3,976,395.33 in canal transit tolls. On her return trip to England, the *Cedar Branch* narrowly avoided a collision with a derelict vessel 28 miles off the canal's Caribbean entrance. The sighting was immediately reported back to Panama in order to warn following ships. The *Cedar Branch* survived in its trade until 1931, when the ship was sold to A. Lusi, Greece, and renamed *Aenos*. Operated by the "Zephyros" Steam Ship Co., the cargo carrier was sunk by an unidentified submarine on 17 October 1940 off the Hebrides Islands.

George Washington

In this very clear but undated photograph, the Norwegian motorship *George Washington* is on a northbound transit near Gamboa. Similar to the *Jutlandia*, the first motorship to transit Panama southbound, the diesel-driven *George Washington* was one of three motor vessels operated by Fred Olsen & Co. between Europe and the west coast of North America. This route drew a number of the world's first motorships because of the abundance of fuel oil at Californian ports. Built in 1916 by Burmeister & Wain, Copenhagen, the 7,093-ton *George Washington* was the largest diesel-driven ship to have used the canal when it made its first transit on 22 December 1916. The freighter was carrying 9,121 tons of coal from Norfolk, Virginia, to Tiburon, California. Discounting the large Norwegian tankers owned by Wilh. Wilhelmsen and operated through the canal by Union Oil, the Fred Olsen & Co. motor vessels represented a major Norwegian flag presence at Panama. In 1921, the time frame for this picture, the three Fred Olsen vessels made 14 transits of the waterway. In almost all cases, the return voyages to Europe were with full cargoes of grain or flour. In 1934 after 18 years of service under the Norwegian flag, the *George Washington* was sold to W.R. Carpenter & Co. Ltd., and renamed *Rabaul*. On 14 May 1941, during a voyage from Newport to Egypt via Cape Town, the motorship was sunk by the German raider *Atlantis* in the South Atlantic. Six months later the *Atlantis* met a similar fate under the guns of the British heavy cruiser HMS *Devonshire* off Brazil.

Lake Elmont

This view of the Cristóbal dry dock and the steamer *Lake Elmont* was taken during January of 1922. The French had built a small 190-foot by 32-foot dry dock at this location in 1886, but it was expanded by the Americans in 1908 to 300 feet by 50 feet. The *Lake Elmont*, measuring 253 feet in length with a 43-foot beam, was one of the larger oceangoing ships able to make use of the enlarged facility. Most customers tended to be canal work craft, submarines from the nearby Coco Solo navy base, or local sailing vessels. In 1933 the Cristóbal dry dock was modified again, this time to 381-feet by 80-feet, with a depth increase of 7.5 feet. The width increase effectively retired the old steam-powered gantry crane, seen here just in front of the *Lake Elmont*; the crane was dismantled and replaced by two new swinging cranes. The *Lake Elmont* was a Lake-class steamer, one of a very large number of similar ships built during World War I. Though of only 2,674 gross registered tons, the small ship supported a crew of well over thirty. Accommodation was cramped; the captain and first officer occupied cabins just under the navigation bridge, while the other deck officers, cooks, mess boys, engineers,and radio operator inhabited the bridge deck. The chief engineer's cabin was just under the port lifeboat. Firemen, coal passers, and sailors were accommodated aft, while the ship's carpenter and bosun shared a small cabin forward. The little steamer survived for a period of only 12 years, going to the breakers at Baltimore, Maryland, in 1931.

WEST CATANACE

224

West Catanace

One of a large number of standard-design freighters produced in U.S. shipyards during and after World War I, the *West Catanace* is representative of American cargo carriers of the period. Built in 1919 by the South Western Shipbuilding Company, San Pedro, the vessel is seen in Pedro Miguel Locks on 1 February 1922 while proceeding from Puget Sound ports to New York with 6,625 tons of lumber on board. The early 1920s saw lumber transits across Panama mushroom because of an increase in U.S. railroad freight rates. The amount of timber transited via the waterway from the Pacific to the Atlantic in 1920 totaled 205,172 tons. By 1921 that amount had increased to 448,087 tons, a growth of 118 percent. The bulk of the lumber, some 346,249 tons, went to U.S. east coast ports, with smaller amounts destined for Europe and the British Isles. Single vessel loads of over 10,000 tons were eventually handled across the isthmus, with Weyerhaeuser Timber Company's steamship *Pomona* setting the record on 17 June 1924. The steamer transited on her way from Everett, Washington, to Baltimore, Maryland, with 10,750 tons of lumber aboard. The *West Catanace*, owned by the Elder Steel Steam Ship Co., Inc., continued in the timber trade until 1924, when the freighter was sold to the Argonaut Steam Ship Co. and renamed *Atlantic*. The vessel was sold again in 1940 and came under the Panamanian flag. Surviving World War II, the cargo ship was renamed *Theodore* in 1947 and finally broken up at Bo'ness, Scotland, during 1952 as the *Archon*.

226

Tisnaren

This undated view shows the 5,747-ton Swedish motorliner *Tisnaren* in Miraflores Locks during a southbound transit. Typical of Scandinavian cargo vessels of the time, the *Tisnaren* was a very clean ship, well built and well taken care of. One of her officers, dressed in white, stands at the bow of the vessel, while several members of the ship's crew watch transit procedures from the railing. Towing locomotives wait with slack lines as the lock's water supply drains to its lower level. In front of the freighter a massive chain guards the lock gate against a possible run-away transit. In the background, and to the right of the cargo vessel's foremast, the canal's astronomical observatory can be seen perched on a small rise. The *Tisnaren* had been built in 1918 by Aktie. Götaverken, Göteborg for Rederiakties Transatlantic. Along with the Johnson Line, this company was one of the main Swedish shipping firms sending vessels through Panama. While Johnson maintained services between Europe and the Pacific ports of North and South America, Rederiakties Transatlantic served the Australasia trade. Southbound, the company's ships would normally load cargoes of coal or sulphur at U.S. Gulf and East Coast ports for discharge in Australia. Northbound, the freight would be more highly varied, including many tropical products from Southeast Asia. The *Tisnaren* served on her route until the coming of World War II. On 19 May 1942, the ship was sunk by the Italian submarine *Cappellini* in the North Atlantic.

228

Port Curtis and Cristobal

An optical illusion? On the last day of 1922 the Panama Canal photographer caught two ships side by side in Gatun Locks. The 8,287-ton British freighter *Port Curtis* had just entered the middle west chamber at low water while the 9,606-ton American cargo-passenger ship *Cristobal* was being moved forward out of the middle east chamber at high water. Both vessels shared a beam measurement of 58 feet. The *Cristobal* was only 39 feet longer than the British ship, yet, because of the difference in lock water levels, it appears to be much larger in this picture. The *Port Curtis*, built in 1920 for the Commonwealth and Dominion Line, was carrying 3,820 tons of general cargo to Brisbane, Australia. The *Cristobal*, built as the *Tremont* in 1902 for the Boston Steamship Company, was transiting with 4,975 tons of coal for discharge at Balboa. At this time British and American ships were the most frequent users of the Panama Canal. The Commonwealth and Dominion Line was sending a ship a month through Panama on its service between New York and Australia, while the Panama Railroad Steamship Line, operator of the *Cristobal*, maintained weekly sailings between the Isthmus and New York. In 1936 the *Port Curtis* was sold to the Downs S.S. Co. and renamed *Tower Dale*. One year later the vessel passed into Finnish control as the *Kronoborg* and under this name was taken over by the Soviet Union at the end of World War II. The *Cristobal*, replaced by a newer ship in 1939, was sold after a period of lay-up to Sociedad La Florida and renamed *Philippa*. The American cargo-passenger liner was reported to have been broken up in 1951 as the *Esmeralda*.

230

Chinampa

The Standard Oil of New Jersey tanker *Chinampa* has just applied power to move out of Pedro Miguel Lock in this early 1920s photograph. Built in 1903 by Palmer's Co. Ltd., Newcastle, the tanker carries old-fashioned anchors forward, one at the ready and one secured. A "black ship," the *Chinampa* was employed in the U.S. intercoastal trade, transporting petroleum from California fields to the United States Gulf and East Coasts. The 6,894-ton tanker had originally been constructed for Deutsch-Amerik Petroleum of Hamburg as the *Prometheus*, but had come under Standard Oil ownership in 1909—first as the *Cushing* and later as the *Chinampa*. At this time American-flag tonnage was taking a dominant position in canal transit figures. Much of the cargo transported was oil. During 1923, in the month of November alone, 145 tankers passed through the canal. This represented 33 percent of all vessels transited, 39 percent of net canal tonnage, and 43 percent of total cargo. Of these ships, 121 were American. The *Chinampa* was sold in 1924 to Italian interests, who renamed the vessel *Americano*. Caught in the port of Tampico at the outbreak of World War II, the tanker was interned by the Mexican government and allocated to Petroleos Mexicanos S.A., who changed the ship's name to *Tuxpam*. On 27 June 1942 the *Tuxpam* was torpedoed and sunk by German submarine U-129 one hundred miles north of Veracruz, Mexico.

Royal Prince and *Kroonland*

Passenger liner and freighter share adjacent locks in this 1923 photograph taken at Gatun. The liner is the 1902-built *Kroonland*, owned by the Panama Pacific Line and transiting from New York to San Francisco with passengers and 1,267 tons of cargo on board. The cargo vessel is Prince Line's *Royal Prince*, bound from the United Kingdom to the Far East. On the foredeck of the *Kroonland*, a makeshift swimming pool can be seen. Both vessels were nearing the age of retirement from their respective companies. The *Royal Prince*, built in 1907 by Short Bros. Ltd., Sunderland, was sold during the following year to Italian interests and given the rather lengthy designation of *Sic Vos Non Vobis*. In 1927 the freighter was renamed again, this time becoming the *Battinen Accame*. The changes in ownership stopped in 1931 when the ship became *Fortunato*. Under this title, the ex-Furness Withy & Company vessel was broken up in Italy during 1932. The *Kroonland*, once the largest American steamship afloat, made her final transit through the canal on 24 June 1925. The 12,760-ton passenger liner was a sister to the *Finland*, both of which were displaced from the Panama route by newer vessels. *Kroonland* had made her maiden transit of the waterway on 2 February 1915, but was returned to transatlantic service after slides closed the canal later that year. In her lifetime the liner made 28 Panama crossings and paid tolls amounting to $255,992.10. In 1927, after delivering cargo on her final sailing from New York to Antwerp, the 25-year old ship was broken up at Genoa, Italy.

Frederic R. Kellogg

In late November of 1923 the West Liria Slide caused vessel transits through the canal to be made convoy-fashion in both directions. This photograph, taken on 28 November 1923 at Empire Moorings, shows the American tanker *Frederic R. Kellogg* proceeding northbound past four southbound ships tied up along the bank. The 7,127-ton *Frederic R. Kellogg*, owned by Huasteca Petroleum Company, was on a voyage from San Pedro, California, to New Orleans with 10,171 tons of crude oil on board. The tanker was being followed in convoy by the American freighter *K.I. Luckenbach*, which was transiting from Seattle to Mobile with 8,000 tons of general cargo. The lead outboard ship of the tied-up vessels is also a Luckenbach freighter, the *J.L. Luckenbach,* which was sailing from Boston to San Pedro with 6,000 tons of general cargo. Inboard of the *J.L. Luckenbach* is the Spanish-flagged *Jupiter*, which was being operated by Companhia Anonima Maritime on a voyage between St.Vincent and Arica in ballast. Also in ballast were the large freighter *British Monarch*, berthed behind the *J.L. Luckenbach*, and the *Mina Brea*, berthed to the rear of the *Jupiter*. The *British Monarch* was on a voyage from Dartmouth to San Pedro, while the *Mina Brea*, fitted as a tanker, was headed for Talara, Peru, from Montreal to load crude oil. All ships pictured were clear of the canal by 11 P.M. that same day. The *Frederic R. Kellogg*, built by Moore & Scott Iron Works, Oakland, California, in 1917, had an exceptionally long life for a petroleum carrier and was not broken up until 1958.

Canada Maru

Owned by Japan's Osaka Shosen Kaisha (O.S.K. Line), the 5,760-ton freighter *Canada Maru* transits southbound on 21 March 1924 carrying 3,131 tons of general cargo from Buenos Aires to Kobe. Disappearing in the background is the 12,257-ton British liner *Oroya* on a voyage between Talcahuano, Chile, and the United Kingdom. At the time of this photograph, British ships were the leading users of the Panama Canal, and in 1924 they totaled 542 transits out of a commercial fleet of 10,078 vessels. The *Canada Maru* was one of 94 Japanese ships to transit Panama that year out of a total national fleet of 2,055 vessels. But Japan was a rising maritime power and by the mid-1920s had become the third largest user of the waterway. In fiscal 1924, Japanese merchant vessels transported 935,245 tons of cargo across the isthmus and paid tolls amounting to $844,976.31. These statistics led the sums tallied by Norway and Germany, but they followed by a wide margin those posted by the United States and Great Britain. The *Canada Maru*, a good example of Japanese merchant tonnage of the period, was built by Mitsubishi at Nagasaki in 1911 and traded under O.S.K. colors for nearly a quarter of a century. In 1935 the ship was sold to Nanyo Kainn K.K., then resold one year later to Miyaji Shoten K.K. In 1937 the *Canada Maru* again changed hands, going first to Kuribayashi K.K., then, in 1939, to Hachiuma K.K., who renamed the vessel *Tamon Maru* No. 5. Sailing under this name on 7 May 1943, the freighter was torpedoed and sunk off Tamagawa, Japan, by the American submarine USS *Wahoo*.

238

Tusitala and *V-1*

On 19 February 1927 warship and sailing ship transit together in Gatun Locks. The three-masted sailing vessel is the 1883-built *Tusitala*, named after the great "Story Teller," Robert Louis Stevenson. On the ship's poop deck her captain can be seen pacing, a deck chair at his disposal. Ahead is the United States submarine *V-1* with canvas awnings spread and many of her crew out on deck. The submarine was returning to Cristóbal from a visit to Panama's Pearl Islands, which she made in company with her sister vessels *V-2*, *V-3*, and the submarine tender *Argonne*. The *Tusitala* was bound from Seattle to New York via Baltimore with 2,500 tons of magnesite and lumber on board. As the last American-flag commercial sailing vessel remaining in operation between the two coasts, the *Tusitala* had developed a regular trade of hauling sulphate of ammonia from New York to Hawaii, then returning to the East Coast from Seattle with a mixed cargo. At this stage the ship was not an economical venture, but she was kept operating by the generosity of her owner, James A. Farrell, president of the U.S. Steel Corporation. Her last voyage through the canal, a northbound transit, was accomplished in early 1932. All totaled, the 1,642-ton *Tusitala* made sixteen transits of the waterway in her lifetime and paid approximately $37,600 in transit and towing charges. In 1945 the *V-1*, which had been renamed *Barracuda* in 1931, was decommissioned and sold for scrap. Although the *Tusitala* was sold to breakers in 1938, the sailing vessel survived for a further decade because of World War II. She was finally dismantled at Mobil, Alabama, in 1948.

City of New York

Like a craft from a different age, the small sailing ship *City of New York* rests in Pedro Miguel Lock on 17 September 1928, as spectators and dignitaries look on. The three-masted bark was the first unit of Commander Richard E. Byrd's 1928 Antarctica Expedition to reach Panama. Forty-three years old at the time, the *City of New York* was a stoutly built ex-whaling vessel that had been finished by K. Larsen of Arendal, Norway, in 1885. She was purchased by Byrd at the suggestion of Roald Amundsen, first man to reach the South Pole. Under the command of Captain Frederick C. Melville, the *City of New York* had departed Hoboken, New Jersey, on 25 August 1928 with 200 tons of supplies and a crew of 20 aboard. A second expedition vessel, the 800-ton steel-hulled cargo ship *Eleanor Bolling*, followed, reaching Panama on October 6th. In addition, two whaling ships, the *James Clark* and *C.A. Larsen*, were assisting the expedition. The *City of New York* departed Balboa for Dunedin, New Zealand, on September 18th, but returned for repairs to its auxiliary coal-burning engine the next day. The vessel eventually reached Bay of Whales, Antarctica, on 28 December 1928. On 1 July 1930, the *City of New York* returned to Panama from Antarctica and after taking on supplies and water, departed for New York under tow of the U.S. Navy tug *Sciota*. The little ship sailed on for many more years, until a fire destroyed the vessel following a grounding off Yarmouth, Nova Scotia, on 30 December 1953.

242

Dean Emery

United States intercoastal traffic was at a peak when this photograph was taken at Pedro Miguel Locks on 14 December 1928. Petroleum movement from California fields to the East Coast, along with passenger movements by scheduled liner services, made up a substantial portion of the traffic. In this view the 6,664-ton tanker *Dean Emery* can be seen in the west lock as the lock chamber is filled with water. Owned by Pan American Petroleum & Transport Company, the 1919-built ship was proceeding from Los Angeles to Baltimore with 9,300 tons of gasoline on board. In the east lock, water is being drained to lower the 10,533-ton *President Hayes* to the level of Miraflores Lake. The American passenger-cargo liner, in round-the-world service under the Dollar Line banner, was transiting from New York to San Francisco with 3,450 tons of general cargo. Behind the *President Hayes*, the Panama-Pacific liner *Virginia* can be seen approaching the lock tie-up mole. Dressed in signal flags, the 20,773-ton *Virginia* was on her maiden voyage to California, having been launched at Newport News on October 18th. All three vessels would go on to serve many more years and survive the destruction of World War II. The *Dean Emery* was eventually broken up in 1949 after operating under both the Panamanian and British flag. The *President Hayes*, an Army transport during the war, followed the tanker to the scrap yards ten years later. The *Virginia*, renamed *Brazil* in 1938, became a troop transport in 1942 and was broken up in 1964 after re-entering commercial service in 1947.

244

Clan Malcolm

On 30 April 1929 the 5,994-ton *Clan Malcolm*, owned by Cayzer, Irvine & Co. Ltd., of the United Kingdom, passed through Panama northbound on a voyage from Australia to England. The 12-knot vessel had been built by Craig Taylor & Co. Ltd., Stockton, during 1917 in a company effort to keep ahead of war losses. Two officers are visible on the stern of the ship, both attired in pith helmets and tropical white uniforms. Ahead, the lock's secondary gate is just beginning to open. Of interest is the adjacent chamber, emptied for overhaul, and the emergency dam swung across the entrance. The dams, which were used to block water while lock gates were overhauled, also furnished accident protection. They functioned by the positioning of a girder frame into iron seatings on the chamber floor. Once the frame was in place, steel plates were lowered along the frame, forming an almost watertight barrier. Fortunately, few accidents happened during canal operations, and the dams were never needed for other than gate repair work. They were eventually dismantled and replaced by floating metal caissons that can be moved in and out of position as required. The *Clan Malcolm* was lost on 27 September 1935 when the vessel slammed into Tregwin Rocks near The Lizard, Cornwall, while on a passage between London and Glasgow in dense fog. A salvage vessel was engaged to pull the ship off, but the freighter held fast and became a total loss. The crew was able to disembark safely.

Point Ancha

A product of Todd Drydock & Construction Company, Tacoma, Washington, the 4,727-ton freighter *Point Ancha* was built in 1919 for the United States Shipping Board as the *Delight*. After its completion, the vessel was operated by several firms, including F. Waterhouse & Company and the Great Southern Redwood Company's "Redwood Line." When the Redwood Line merged with the Gulf Pacific Line in 1931, the *Delight* came under Swayne & Hoyt management and was renamed *Point Ancha*. Swayne & Hoyt Inc. had been set up at the turn of the century by Robert H. Swayne and John G. Hoyt and was a respected name in the west coast lumber industry. Shortly after taking over operation of the *Point Ancha*, the firm gained an important U.S. government mail contract. In order to fulfill the various requirements of this contract, the *Point Ancha* was sent to the Long Beach Shipbuilding Company's yard at Long Beach, California, for extensive modifications. This involved work on the vessel's machinery, rudder, and the fitting of limited passenger accommodation. The *Point Ancha* then began operating in Swayne & Hoyt's Gulf Pacific Mail Line service between the North American west coast and Caribbean ports. This undated photograph, showing the freighter in Miraflores Locks with a deck cargo of lumber, was probably taken in mid-1931, not long after the cargo ship came under Swayne & Hoyt control. In 1940 the *Point Ancha* was sold to A. G. Papadakis of Romania, who renamed the vessel *Macon*. Under this name, the ship was torpedoed and sunk by a submarine on 24 July 1941 just west of Madeira island.

248

Jacob Rupert

On 31 October 1933 a rusty-looking tramp passed through Panama with an odd collection of cargo and a unique destination: Antarctica. The ship was the 5,645-ton *Jacob Rupert*, which was transporting supplies and equipment for the Second Byrd Antarctic Expedition. The 13-year-old freighter had been leased by Byrd from the United States Shipping Board for one dollar per year and after having been reconditioned at Boston, had left that port on October 11th. The cargo vessel was proceeding to Antarctica in company with the 1874-built *Bear of Oakland*, a 705-ton ex-U.S. government cutter that was to be Byrd's main exploration vessel. The *Jacob Rupert* was under the command of Lieutenant W.F. Verleger, USNR. Visible on the ship's after deck is the expedition's largest aircraft, a partially disassembled Curtiss-Wright Condor, which Byrd had named the "William Horlick." The *Jacob Rupert* was also transporting three smaller aircraft, two Ford snowmobiles, a Cletrac Tractor, and three Citroen vehicles, as well as a sizable yacht for use as a tender. Built in 1920 by Western Pipe & Steel Company, San Francisco, as the *West Cahokia*, the freighter had spent most of her life transporting lumber. Though not designed for Arctic use, the old steamer proved her worth by successfully delivering Byrd's exploration equipment to the ice and returning through the canal in April of 1935 with most of the machinery still intact. In 1941 the *Jacob Rupert* was sold to the North Atlantic Transport Company and renamed *Cocle*. Under this name the vessel was torpedoed and sunk on 12 May 1942 by German submarine U-94, north of the Azore Islands.

Appendixes

A

First Transits of the Panama Canal

The first transit of the Panama Canal by a self-propelled vessel was made by the craneboat *Alexandre La Valley* on 7 January 1914. The former French craneboat had been used at the Atlantic entrance of the canal, but was moved to Gaillard Cut (then known as Culebra Cut) for excavation work. After completing its task, the craneboat was sent on to the Pacific side rather than back to Cristóbal, thus completing a full ocean-to-ocean transit. On 1 February 1914 the tug *Reliance* became the first vessel to use the canal northbound when, having circumnavigated South America, it passed through Gatun Locks on its way to Cristóbal. The tug had previously sailed from Cristóbal on 11 February 1912 for Balboa via the Strait of Magellan and had arrived at Balboa on 17 June 1912.

On 18 May 1914, three barges loaded with sugar, transferred to them at Balboa from the steamer *Alaskan*, were towed as far as the lower end of Pedro Miguel Locks; their transit, after a change of towboats, was completed at 9 P.M. on 19 May 1914. This was the first handling of a commercial cargo through the canal. On 19 May 1914, the tug *Mariner* towed two empty barges

through the canal from Cristóbal to Balboa, arriving at 6:40 P.M. that same day. This was the first direct or continuous southbound voyage of a vessel through the canal from ocean to ocean.

In anticipation of the opening of the canal, a test voyage from Cristóbal to Balboa was made by the steamship *Cristobal* of the Panama Railroad Steamship Line on 3 August 1914, and a return trip was made on 4 August. The *Advance*, of the same line, was sent from the Atlantic to the Pacific and back again as far as Gatun Locks on 9 August 1914, completing the transit on 10 August. The *Panama* made a similar trip on 11 August, completing the return transit on August 12. Guest passengers were carried on these trips, but no cargo was handled. These were the first passenger-ship transits.

The *Ancon* of the Panama Railroad Steamship Line was sent through the canal from Cristóbal to Balboa on 15 August 1914, carrying cargo for transshipment at Balboa and about 200 passengers who were invited by the U.S. Secretary of War. This is considered the first transit of an oceangoing steamship in commercial service. The ship discharged cargo at Balboa and returned through the canal to Cristóbal on 23 August 1914. On 15 August 1914, following the departure of the *Ancon*, transit of the canal was begun by the steamship *Arizonan* of the American-Hawaiian Line, leaving Cristóbal at 10:23 A.M. This vessel completed its transit the following day, passing Balboa at 4:10 P.M. 16 August 1914. The *Arizonan* carried 11,183 tons of cargo and was the first merchant vessel to use the canal on a voyage between ports beyond the canal terminals.

The yacht *Lasata*, owned by Morgan Adams, followed the *Arizonan* through the canal, beginning its transit at 1:00 P.M. on August 15th and completing its transit at 5:35 P.M. on the 17th. This was the first transit of the canal by a private yacht.

On 16 August 1914 the freighter *Pleiades* of the Luckenback Steamship Company departed Balboa at 6:50 A.M. and arrived at Cristóbal by 5:30 P.M. the same day, thus becoming the first northbound commercial transit. The vessel was carrying 5,400 tons of general cargo on a voyage from San Francisco to New York.

The first non-American vessel to transit the canal, and the first warship of any nation, was the Peruvian gunboat *Teniente Rodriguez*. The gunboat arrived at Colón on 16 August 1914 and passed through the canal on August 18. The 460-ton French-built vessel had been on a trip up the Amazon River as far as the port of Iquitos, Peru, and was returning to Callao, Peru.

The first non-American-flag merchant vessel to transit the canal was the British-registered *Daldorch*, a cargo steamer belonging to J. and M. Campbell of Glasgow, Scotland. The ship had left Tacoma, Washington with 11,500 tons of wheat on the day of the outbreak of hostilities in Europe. The freighter arrived at Balboa on 20 August 1914 and passed through the canal bound for Limerick, Ireland, on August 22nd.

The first United States military vessel to transit the canal was the U.S. Army transport *Buford*, which arrived at Balboa from San Francisco on 6 September 1914 and passed through the canal on its way to Galveston, Texas, on September 9th.

The first United States Navy ship to transit the canal was the collier *Jupiter*, coming from the Pacific Ocean on 10 October 1914 and transiting to Philadelphia, Pennsylvania.

The first commercial motorship to transit the canal, and also the first Swedish ship, was the Johnson Line's *Kronprinzessin Margareta*, which passed through the waterway on 18 October 1914 during a voyage from Valparaiso, Chile, to Malmö, Sweden with 5,987 tons of nitrates on board.

The first commercial sailing ship to transit the canal was the 132-foot British-registered schooner *Zeta* owned by Robert Wilcox. The *Zeta* transited on 28 November 1914 with 600 tons of lumber on board during a voyage from Gulfport, Mississippi, to Panama City, Panama.

The First Vessels by Nationality Passing through the Panama Canal from Its Opening through March 1941

The following list was compiled by Nan S. Chong, Panama Canal Collection Librarian at the Panama Canal Library, Balboa, from the "Movements of Ocean Vessels" column appearing in the official Panama Canal publication *Canal Record*. It gives first vessel transits of the Panama Canal according to nationality from August 1914 through March 1941 when the *Canal Record* ceased publication because of World War II. It does not include the time period 9 February 1917 through 7 December 1918 when, as a security measure during World War I, "Movements of Ocean Vessels" was not published. During this blackout period it is known that vessels of Chinese, Greek, Belgian, Colombian, Ecuadoran, and Uruguayan nationality used the canal.

Notes on First Vessel Transits by Nationality

Following the transit of the Peruvian warship *Teniente Rodriguez*, the first Peruvian commercial transit of the Panama Canal was by the small passenger-cargo liner *Urubamba*, en route from Cardiff to Mollendo with 2,000 tons of coal on 8 November 1914.

The Danish vessel *Transvaal* was on a voyage between San Francisco and Europe with 7,082 tons of grain when it made its first transit.

The first Dutch ship through the waterway, the *J.B. Aug. Kessler,* was carrying 8,142 tons of refined petroleum between Port Arthur, Texas, and Tien Tsin, China.

The first Norwegian vessel to transit the canal, *Capella I*, was also the first whaling ship to transit. The vessel was transporting 3,400 tons of whale oil to Sandfjord, Norway, and was accompanied by its three 100-ton whale-catching craft *Hidalgo, Juarez,* and *Morelos.*

The *Wilhelmina*, the first Nicaraguan vessel to use the canal, was a 66-ton motor schooner that brought six tons of stores belonging to the Nicaraguan government to Balboa for transshipment. The vessel then returned through the canal to Bluefields on the eastern coast of Nicaragua with 45 tons of sugar. For many months it remained the smallest vessel to have used the canal on a commercial basis.

Nationality	Ship	Date
American	*Ancon*	15 August 1914
Peruvian	*Teniente Rodriguez*	18 August 1914
British	*Daldorch*	22 August 1914
Danish	*Transvaal*	31 August 1914
Dutch	*J.B. Aug. Kessler*	24 September 1914
Norwegian	*Capella I*	25 September 1914
Swedish	*Kronprinzessin Margareta*	18 October 1914
Nicaraguan	*Wilhelmina*	13 November 1914
Chilean	*Limari*	2 December 1914
Japanese	*Tokushima Maru*	10 December 1914
Panamanian	*Chitre*	11 January 1915
Russian	*Baron Driesen*	17 January 1915
Honduran	*Bertha E. May*	2 March 1915
French	*Saint Andre*	16 March 1915
Italian	*Vega*	19 March 1915
Canadian	*Durley Chine*	17 May 1915
Argentinian	*Presidente Sarmiento*	14 July 1915
Mexican	*Pinotepa*	23 July 1916
Costa Rican	*Izabal*	9 September 1916
Spanish	*Carlos*	21 September 1916
Cuban	*Jalisco*	23 October 1916
Brazilian	*Ayuruoca*	18 November 1919
German	*Schelde*	2 January 1920
Portuguese	*Goa*	5 February 1920
Yugoslavian	*Jugoslaven Prvi*	9 July 1920
Finnish	*Milverton*	26 April 1921
Danzig Free State	*Vistula*	5 February 1924
Irish	*Westwego*	27 July 1924
Venezuelan	*Apure*	4 July 1932
Polish	*Dar Pomorza*	27 November 1934
Hungarian	*Csarda*	7 November 1935
Estonian	*Eestirand*	27 November 1936
Latvian	*Rasma*	10 February 1937
Philippine	*Don Jose*	19 June 1937
Egyptian	*Star of Alexandria*	1 September 1939
Rumanian	*Siretul*	15 February 1940
Thailand	*Suriyothai Nawa*	27 December 1940

The first Chilean vessel to use the canal, the passenger-cargo steamer *Limari*, also became the first vessel to use the canal at night when it was granted special authority for a night lockage through Miraflores and Pedro Miguel Locks on 7 December 1914. The ship had just inaugurated a new service for the South American Steamship Company (Compañia Sud Americana de Vapores) and was returning from Cristóbal to Valparaiso, Chile.

The first Japanese ship to use the canal, the *Tokushima Maru*, was owned by Nippon Yusen Kaisha Line. The vessel was transporting 15,062 bales (4,000 tons) of cotton from Galveston, Texas, to Yokohama, Japan. Though the crew of the ship was Japanese, the vessel's captain and chief officers were British.

The first Panamanian craft to pass through the canal, the *Chitre*, was a patrol vessel of the Panamanian government and thus was exempt from paying a transit toll. It was the first vessel to transit the canal free of charge in acordance with Article XIX of the 19 November 1903 treaty between the United States and the Republic of Panama. This article gave the Panamanian government the right to transport over the canal its vessels and its troops and munitions of war without paying charges of any kind. The 241-ton *Chitre* had originally been built in Millwall, England, by Edwards and Company, Ltd., as the *Lillian* for the Panama Steamship Company. The first Panamanian commercial vessel to use the waterway was the small 15-ton passenger launch *La Pilarica* owned by Manuel Alonzo; it crossed the isthmus on 23 April 1915.

The first Russian ship to use the canal, the *Baron Driesen*, was proceeding from Savannah, Georgia, to

Vladivostok, Siberia, with 5,566 tons of cotton and nitrates aboard.

The first Honduran vessel through the waterway, the *Bertha E. May* owned by H.R. Wood, was a 74-ton sailing schooner that crossed from Colón to Panama City in ballast.

The first Canadian ship to transit the canal, the *Durley Chine*, also passed through in ballast. The vessel was bound from Halifax to Vancouver, B.C., and was being operated by the Alum Chine S.S. Co.

The first Italian vessel to use the canal, the *Vega*, had on board 900 tons of material for the Italian government's exhibit at the Panama-Pacific International Exposition at San Francisco. The ship returned from San Francisco on May 7th and transited in ballast for Galveston, Texas.

The first Argentinian ship to pass through Panama, the *Presidente Sarmiento*, was also the first naval training vessel to use the waterway. The vessel was proceeding from Acajutla, El Salvador, to Havana, Cuba.

The first Mexican vessel to cross the isthmus, the 452-ton *Pinotepa*, was being operated by the Pacific Steam Navigation Company on a voyage between Salina Cruz and Cristóbal with 172 tons of hides and coffee on board.

The first Costa Rican steamship to use the waterway, the *Izabal,* had originally been used by the Pacific Mail Line to haul water from Taboga Island to ships calling at Balboa. After her sale to the owners of a manganese mine in Costa Rica, the vessel was converted to a miniature ore carrier. On her first crossing to the Atlantic she had on board 200 tons of manganese and lead for transshipment at Cristóbal.

The first ship under the Spanish flag to make use of the canal, the *Carlos*, was owned by Juan L. Prado and Son and was on a voyage from Norfolk, Virginia, to Mejillones, Chile, with 3,391 tons of coal.

The first Cuban ship through the canal, the *Jalisco*, inaugurated a new passenger-cargo service by the New York and Cuban Mail Steamship Company between New York and Salina Cruz, Mexico, by way of Havana and the west coast ports of Central America. The 2,841-ton ship brought 32 passengers and 1,400 tons of general cargo to the isthmus on this voyage.

The first Brazilian ship through the canal, the 9,061-ton *Ayuruoca*, is recorded as having been chartered by the French government for a voyage between Norfolk, Virginia, and Iquique, Chile, in ballast.

The first oceangoing German vessel to transit the canal under the German flag, the tug *Schelde*, was transiting in company with a second German tug, the *Einigkeit*. Both vessels were on their way from Hamburg to Valparaiso under British Admiralty orders to tow disabled German vessels from Chilean ports back to England for overhaul. Prior to the passage of these two craft, both sailing with German crews, the small launch *Germania* passed between Cristóbal and Balboa flying the German flag. A number of German ships had also transited earlier as war prizes, including the freighter *Dusseldorf* and the submarine *B-88*, but none under the German flag.

The first Portuguese vessel to transit the canal, the *Goa,* was owned by the Portuguese government and operated by Transportes Maritimes de Estado. The 6,409-ton ship was carrying 4,000 tons of general cargo between New York and Valparaiso via Callao and Mollendo.

The first Yugoslavian vessel through the canal, the

3,125-ton *Jugoslaven Prvi,* was on a similar routing, taking 4,025 tons of coal from Newport News to Arica, Chile.

The first Finnish ship to use the waterway, the 2,250-ton *Milverton,* was returning from Antofagasta, Chile, to Falmouth for orders with 3,490 tons of nitrate.

The first vessel of the Danzig Free State (today part of Poland) to cross Panama, the tankship *Vistula,* was owned by the Baltisch Amerikanische Petroleum Import Co. of Danzig and was traveling in ballast from Baton Rouge, Louisiana, to Los Angeles. Two other tankers flying the same flag, the *Gedania* and *Baltic,* followed the *Vistula.* All three ships were under charter to the Standard Oil Company of New Jersey.

The first Irish vessel to use the canal, the *Westwego,* was also a tanker under charter. The ship was owned by the Irish-American Oil Company and sailing between Liverpool and San Francisco in ballast while under charter to the Anglo-American Oil Company. The *Westwego* had made several previous transits of the canal under the United States flag when her owners were the Union Petroleum Steamship Company.

The first Venezuelan ship to cross Panama did so free of charge. The tanker *Apure,* owned by the Venezuela Gulf Oil Company, was proceeding in ballast from Maracaibo, Venezuela, to Balboa for dry-docking. Under canal regulations in effect at the time, a ship transiting for repair work at canal workshops, then returning directly back through the canal, was not assessed transit charges.

The first Polish ship to enter the canal was the famous training ship *Dar Pomorza,* which was circling the globe on a world cruise with several hundred naval cadets on board.

The first Hungarian vessel to pass through Panama, the *Csarda,* was traveling from Iquique, Chile, to the Azore Islands for orders with 6,020 tons of nitrates on board.

The first ship of Estonian registry to transit the canal, the *Eestirand,* was proceeding from Flushing, Holland, to Taltal, Chile, in ballast to load a cargo of nitrate for the Chile Nitrate Sales Corporation.

The same case was true for the first vessel of Latvian registry to enter the canal, the 1902-built *Rasma.* Owned by the Latvian State Shipping Board of Riga, Latvia, the coal-burning *Rasma* was en route from Wilmington, North Carolina, to Tocopilla, Chile, for a cargo of nitrates.

The first vessel to carry the flag of the Philippines through Panama, the Madrigal & Company's *Don Jose,* was on a voyage from New York to Manila with 15,414 tons of pig iron and general cargo on board.

The first Egyptian ship through the waterway, the *Star of Alexandria,* was carrying 7,350 tons of nitrates from Tocopilla, Chile, to Alexandria, Egypt, under charter to the Chile Nitrate Sales Corporation.

The first Rumanian vessel to use the Panama canal, the *Siretul,* was also carrying nitrates, a load of 6,181 tons, bound from Iquique,Chile, to Genoa, Italy.

The first ship to cross Panama flying the flag of Thailand, the *Suriyothai Nawa,* was transporting 4,098 tons of rice from Bangkok to La Guaira, Venezuela.

C

A Comparison of the Panama and Suez Canals

The world's two great interocean canals, Panama and Suez, have often been compared. Though cut through vastly different terrain, both waterways run north and south to connect seas that lie to the east and west. One of the oddities in comparing the two canals is the fact that the original plans for both were changed. Suez was first planned as a lock canal, but became a sea-level route. Original plans for the Panama Canal called for a sea-level channel, but it became the world's largest lock canal. The Suez Canal was opened on 17 November 1869. The Panama Canal opened on 15 August 1914. To create the Suez Canal, approximately 97,000,000 cubic yards of earth were excavated at a cost of around $148,500,000. At Panama, approximately 262,000,000 cubic yards were excavated at a cost of almost $640,000,000 (total cost of both French and American projects).

In 1924 after ten years of operation, the Panama Canal was handling approximately the same number of ships and the same volume of cargo as Suez. Figures for that year show that 5,122 vessels totaling 25,109,921 net registered tons moved through Suez with 25,529,000 tons of cargo. During the same period, 4,893 ships totaling 24,411,760 net registered tons transited the Panama Canal carrying 25,892,134 tons of cargo. Traffic through the Panama Canal, excepting cargo tonnage, was slightly less in 1924 than in 1923. Traffic through the Suez canal during 1924 was approximately 10 percent greater than in 1923.

In the Suez records, barges and miscellaneous craft of less than 300 tons measurement were omitted from the traffic statistics, while the Panama Canal traffic statistics include such vessels if over 20 tons. A number of naval vessels were included in the Suez statistics, while in those of Panama, transits of United States naval vessels, army transports, and other public vessels of the United States (which numbered 403 transits in 1924) were omitted.

In 1936 a similar comparison survey of the two canals was taken that showed 4,858 ships passing through Suez during the first ten months of the year and 4,778 ships passing through Panama. By early 1939, largely on account of increased petroleum cargo movements, the Suez Canal started to pull ahead of the Panama Canal in numbers of ships and volume of cargo handled. Today the Suez Canal, which was extensively dredged and widened in the years 1975–80, enjoys a clear superiority in ship and cargo-handling statistics. In 1983 the Suez Canal transited 22,224 ships and 256,705,000 tons of cargo, compared to 13,293 ships and 145,949,000 tons of cargo handled through Panama.*

*Figures provided by the Panama Canal Commission Records Management Branch, Balboa, Republic of Panama, based on fiscal year. Figures provided by the Suez Canal Authority Information and Microfilm Systems Centre, Ismaila, Arab Republic of Egypt, based on calendar year.

D

Canal Traffic by Fiscal Years 1915–1939

Comparative traffic statistics covering oceangoing vessels for each fiscal year since the Panama Canal was opened for navigation through fiscal 1939 are shown in the following table:

Year	Number of transits	Panama Canal net tonnage*	Tolls	Tons of cargo
1915	†1,058	3,507,000	$4,366,747.13	4,888,400
1916	‡ 724	2,212,000	$2,403,089.40	3,093,335
1917	1,738	5,357,000	$5,620,799.83	7,054,720
1918	1,989	6,072,000	$6,428,780.26	7,525,768
1919	1,948	5,658,000	$6,164,290.79	6,910,097
1920	2,393	7,898,000	$8,507,938.68	9,372,374
1921	2,791	10,550,000	$11,268,681.46	11,595,971
1922	2,665	10,556,000	$11,191,828.56	10,882,607
1923	3,908	17,206,000	$17,504,027.19	19,556,429
1924	5,158	24,181,000	$24,284,659.92	26,993,167
1925	4,592	21,134,000	$21,393,718.01	23,956,549
1926	5,087	22,906,000	$22,919,931.89	26,030,016
1927	5,293	24,245,000	$24,212,250.61	27,733,555
1928	6,253	27,229,000	$26,922,200.75	29,615,651
1929	6,289	27,585,000	$27,111,125.47	30,647,768
1930	6,027	27,716,000	$27,059,998.94	30,018,429
1931	5,370	25,690,000	$24,624,599.76	25,065,283
1932	4,362	21,842,000	$20,694,704.61	19,798,986
1933	4,162	21,094,000	$19,601,077.17	18,161,165
1934	5,234	26,410,000	$24,047,183.44	24,704,009
1935	5,180	25,720,000	$23,307,062.93	25,309,527
1936	5,382	25,923,000	$23,479,114.21	26,505,943
1937	5,387	25,430,000	$23,102,137.12	28,108,375
1938	6,524	25,950,383	$23,169,888.70	27,385,924
1939	5,903	27,170,007	$23,661,021.08	27,866,627

*Panama Canal net tonnages prior to 1939 are estimated figures based on revised measurement rules that became effective 1 March 1938.

†Canal opened to traffic 15 August 1914.

‡Canal closed to traffic approximately 7 months of fiscal year by slides (18 September 1915 to 14 April 1916).

E

Panama Canal Transit Records*

Record	Ship	Last Transit Date
Length		
972.68 feet	*San Juan Prospector*	6 April 1973
Beam		
108.2 feet	U.S. Navy *Iowa*-class battleships (*Iowa, Missouri, New Jersey*)	30 August 1984 (*Iowa*)
Panama Canal Net Tonnage		
56,877 tons	*San Juan Prospector*	6 April 1973
Tolls		
$99,065.22	*Queen Elizabeth 2*	20 January 1985
Cargo		
65,299 long tons	*Arco Texas*	15 December 1981

*(as of 1 July 1985)

Bibliography

Books

Bates, Lindon W. *Retrieval at Panama*. New York, 1907.

Burchell, S.C. *Building of the Suez Canal*. New York: American Heritage Publishing Co., Inc., 1966.

Charles, Roland. *Troopships of World War II*. Washington, D.C.: Army Transport Assn., 1947.

Chesneau, Roger, ed. *Conway's All the World's Fighting Ships*, 1922–1946. London: Conway Maritime Press, 1980.

Chesneau, Roger, and Eugene M. Kolesnik, eds. *All the World's Fighting Ships*, 1860–1905. New York: Mayflower Books, 1979.

Claybourne, John G. *Dredging of the Panama Canal, 1913*. Paper presented at the first meeting of the Panama Section of the American Society of Civil Engineers held at Panama City, Republic of Panama, on 27 February 1931.

Dunn, Laurence. *Famous Liners of the Past, Belfast Built*. Southampton: Adlard Coles, 1964.

Dunn, Laurence. *Passenger Liners*. Southampton: Adlard Coles, 1961–1965.

Emmons, Frederick. *The Atlantic Liners 1925–1970*. New York: Bonanza Books.

Gause, Frank A., and Charles C. Carr. *The Story of Panama, The New Route to India*. Silver, Burdett and Co. 1912.

Hansen, Hans Jurgen. *The Ships of the German Fleets 1848–1945*. New York: Arco Publishing Co., 1975.

Hansgeorg, Jentschura, Dieter Jung, and Peter Mickel. *Warships of the Imperial Japanese Navy 1869–1945*. Annapolis: Naval Institute Press, 1977.

Hartman, Tom. *The Guinness Book of Ships and Shipping Facts and Feats*. Enfield: Guinness Superlatives, 1983.

Hocking, Charles. *Dictionary of Disasters at Sea During the Age of Steam 1824–1962*. London: Lloyd's Register of Shipping, 1969.

Hofman, Erik. *The Steam Yachts*. 1970.

Kirwan, Laurence P. *A History of Polar Exploration*. New York: W.W. Norton, 1959.

Kludas, Arnold. *Great Passenger Ships of the World*. Vols. 1–5. Cambridge, England: Patrick Stephens, 1977.

Lyon, Hugh, J. *The Encyclopedia of the World's Warships: A Technical Directory of Major Fighting Ships from 1900 to the Present Day*. New York: Crescent Books, 1978.

McCullough, David. *The Path Between the Seas*. New York: Simon and Schuster, 1977.

McKeller, Tamworth. *Steel Shipbuilding under the U.S.*

Shipping Board 1917–1921. Unpublished manuscript from the collection of the Steamship Historical Society of America, University of Baltimore, Baltimore.

Melville, John H. *The Great White Fleet*. New York: Vantage Press, Inc., 1976.

Newell, Gordon. *Ocean Liners of the 20th Century*. New York: Bonanza Books, 1973.

Pepperman, W. Leon. *Who Built the Panama Canal*. New York: E.P. Dutton & Co., 1915.

Reilly, John, and Robert Scheina. *American Battleships 1886–1923*. Annapolis: Naval Institute Press, 1980.

Smith, Eugene. *Passenger Ships of the World Past and Present*. Boston: George H. Dean Company, 1978.

Stindt, Fred A. *Matson's Century of Ships*. Modesto, CA: Fred A. Stindt, 1982.

Taffrail. *Blue Star Line at War 1939–1945*. London: W. Foulsham & Co., 1973.

Taylor, John Charles. *German Warships of World War I*. New York: Doubleday, 1970.

Tinnan, Oleta. *Short History of the Panama Canal Graphic Branch*. Unpublished draft manuscript prepared for the "Panama Canal Review." Panama Canal Commission, Balboa, Republic of Panama.

Winchester, Clarence, ed. *Shipping Wonders of the World*. Vols. 1 & 2. London: Amalgamated Press, 1939.

Magazine Articles

Nielson, Jon M. "The American Dreadnoughts 1890–1916." *Sea Classics*.

Pittee, Charles R. "The Panama Railroad Company's Steamship Lines." *Steamboat Bill* (Spring 1964): 9–16.

Miller, Willis M. "Meet S.S. Allianca." *Steamboat Bill* (Winter 1980): 231–34.

Miller, S.J.F. "Allan Line's Alsatian and Calgarian of 1914 of the Canadian Service." *Marine News* (September 1984): 501–502.

"Casa Grace." *Fortune Magazine* (December, 1935): 95–101, 157–58, 161–62, 164.

Newspapers

Panama Times, 6 May 1930.
New York Times, 28 December 1932.
Swedish Shipping Gazette, No.50, 16 December 1937.

Panama Canal Collection Publications

Annual Reports of the Panama Railroad Company. Washington, D.C.: Panama Canal Commission.

Annual Reports of the Panama Canal. Washington, D.C.: Panama Canal Commission.

The Panama Canal 50th Anniversary 1914–1964. Balboa: Panama Canal Information Office, 1964.

Nicaragua Canal. Report of the Nicaragua Canal Board, Document 279 of the 54th Congress, 1st Session, House of Representatives. 1895/96. Washington D.C.: Panama Canal Commission.

Panama Canal Review. Official Panama Canal Publication. Balboa Heights, Panama.

The Panama Canal Record. Official Panama Canal Publication.

Canal Record. Official Panama Canal Publication. Panama.

Serial Titles

Janes Fighting Ships, 1898–1984. Annual.
Lloyds Register of Shipping.
Dictionary of American Naval Fighting Ships.

Index

Note: The dates in parentheses represent the year in which the ships were launched.